MW00935168

LAYERS *of* SILENCE

M.L. CURTIS

Copyright © 2019 M.L. Curtis
All rights reserved
First Edition

PAGE PUBLISHING, INC.
Conneaut Lake, PA

First originally published by Page Publishing 2019

ISBN 978-1-64544-088-8 (pbk)
ISBN 978-1-64544-089-5 (digital)

Printed in the United States of America

Chapter 1

hat the hell am I doing here? Daphne thought. She was sitting in a folding chair inside a crowded gymnasium. Her arms were crossed and her right leg bobbed up and down anxiously. People from all around kept making eye contact. She nodded and smiled bravely despite her discomfort.

Why are they looking at me?!

Relax. They're just being friendly.

No. That's not it. They know.

How could they possibly know?!

They just do. I'm an impostor and they know it. They can see right through me... I never should have come. I should have driven away while I had the chance.

Daphne had that chance while she sat in the parking lot for twenty minutes with the engine of her black Mustang running. She stalled by checking her appearance in the mirror. Her porcelain skin glowed in the late afternoon sun, still baring the subtle scarring of her teen years and early twenties burdened by acne. After a decade of exfoliation, the scars were negligible with just a thin layer of makeup, but Daphne was still painfully aware of them.

With her eyes fixed on her reflection, she curled her upper lip over her gumline. *No food between my teeth...* She closed her mouth and pressed her full lips together. *I could use some more lip balm.* Quickly, she grabbed her handbag from the passenger seat. Her hand fumbled through its contents—a pack of gum, old receipts, a comb... Finally, she felt what could only be a tube of tinted lip balm.

Daphne unscrewed the cap and applied the color to both lips. When she dropped her glance, she noticed her slender nose was shiny. Once again, she rummaged through the inside of her purse. This time, she pulled out her compact. She rubbed the pressed powder down her nose with multiple strokes and then continued over the rest of her face to even out the tone. She examined her face one last time.

It'll have to do, I guess.

The car clock hit 4:25 p.m.

She checked her French-manicured nails. *No chips. No breaks. Good. ...The meeting is going to start soon. I'd hate to be late. People will think I'm incompetent.*

Suddenly, she could hear Renee's voice in her head, clear as a bell: "*You always did care too much about what other people think.*"

Daphne cracked a little smile. *Renee's right. She's always right.*

4:27 p.m.

Now or never, Daphne.

She took a deep breath and turned off the engine. The car was suddenly still and silent. All she heard was the sound of her boot heels as they hit the pavement. She threw her handbag over her shoulder, locked the door from the inside, and stood up.

The warm autumn breeze made her hazelnut hair beat against her cheeks. She took a few steps toward the building before she locked the vehicle once more with the clicker over her shoulder. Her heels clipped with a sense of urgency all the way up to the gymnasium door.

The forty-year-old building bore rust stains and chipped paint. A playground stood adjacent to the center on the other side of the street. Daphne saw parents with their small children on the jungle gym. Others sat on the edge of the sandbox and watched their toddlers try to shovel sand into their pails but dowsing it into their laps instead. The sight made her snicker.

The bulletin board at the entrance door read "Tuesday Night: ACDP meeting at 4:30."

* * *

It was now 4:35 p.m.

Ugh! I guess I didn't have to worry about looking bad. They're not even starting on time. They'd better not run past five thirty. Otherwise, the traffic will be murder on the way to the hospital.

The quiet roar of conversation died, and all eyes turned to the stage. Ruth—a short, pudgy woman in her sixties—stood before them. She had brown hair with a few strands of gray and white around her temples. Her glasses made her pretty blue eyes sparkle, and her kind motherly smile gave Daphne comfort.

"Good evening," she began.

"Good evening," said the crowd.

"Welcome to our meeting for Adult Children of Deceased Parents. We'll open up tonight with our dedication." Ruth proceeded to recite the famous Serenity Prayer. "Lord, grant me the serenity to accept the things I cannot change…"

With those words, Daphne's thoughts began to wander. *I can't change what's happening to Renee. I know that. As for the courage to change the things I can change? I'm not sure I have that either. The wisdom to know the difference? I used to know the difference, or so I thought. Now? I don't know anything anymore.*

"Forever in the next," Ruth said. "Amen."

"Amen," said the audience.

Daphne sat up straighter. *Okay, no more sidebar thoughts. Pay attention!*

Ruth then invited previous speakers to share updates on their progress. At first, no one volunteered.

Oh crap! Daphne thought. *Don't ask if there are any new visitors… please!*

After what was probably ten seconds, an elderly man in the third row with white hair raised his hand. The audience applauded. He stood and sauntered up the steps to the stage and took his place behind the podium.

"Well, my name's Paul."

"Hello, Paul," said the group.

"So as some of you know, I lost my father about five years ago. He was ninety-two at the time. He'd been living in a nursing home for about a year then. My sisters, my brother, and I had been taking turns visiting him every day." He paused for a moment and cleared his throat. "There were a lot of things my dad and I didn't do when he was alive. I don't think we ever hugged. We never said 'I love you.' Humor and sarcasm—that's how we coped with uncomfortable situations. I was fine with that. Then one morning, I got a call from one of the nurses at the home saying that my father wasn't doing well and…we should all come as soon as possible. I called my brother and sisters to meet me there, and they all agreed. But before any of us got there, he was gone."

Daphne could feel her eyes moisten. She took a deep breath and grabbed her handbag from the floor. As quietly as she could, she searched for a pouch of tissues, pulled one out and dabbed her eyes.

"I felt *numb* at first," Paul said. His eyes filled with tears. "And that went on for a couple of *years*. It's like I tried to continue our family tradition of not dealing with stuff. And then I just became angry as hell. I lashed out at my wife of over forty years, even though she did nothing wrong. I didn't want to see my kids or my grandkids. I kept making up excuses not to be around people because I didn't want them to see me."

"Why not?" Ruth asked from her corner at the end of the stage.

"Because I *hated* myself," sobbed Paul. "I hated myself for hating my father after he had *died*! I mean, what kind of son did that make *me*?"

"Why did you hate him?" Ruth asked.

Paul took a long, deep breath before he answered. "I hated him for never saying 'I love you' to me…to *any* of us. I hated him for not wanting us to hug or show emotion or talk things out. I guess I really *needed* those things. He never even said that he was proud of me for any of my accomplishments."

"And now?" asked Ruth.

Paul wiped his tears away. "Now…I've learned that I *can* give others what I didn't have as a child, or even as a grown man. I can tell *my* children and *my* grandchildren that I love them. We can hug and be silly with each other, and it's not a betrayal to my dad." His eyes dropped. A peaceful kind of sadness washed over his face. "I can't change the past. My father was a good man who probably did the best he could. All I can do is honor him by remembering what I loved about him and share that with my family now."

"Sounds like you've made some great progress," said Ruth.

The audience applauded.

He smiled and walked over to shake Ruth's hand, which turned into a hug, making the audience clap even louder.

Daphne sighed deeply and dabbed her eyes one last time.

As Paul slowly made his way back to his seat, Ruth returned to the podium. "Who's next?"

* * *

After the meeting, Daphne made a beeline for the door. The used tissue, which she had rolled into a ball, was still clutched in her hand. She quickly spotted a trash can by the refreshment table and threw the tissue overhand like a basketball. It landed perfectly inside the receptacle. A woman who had been standing nearby noticed and smiled at her. Daphne smiled back and strutted out of the gymnasium.

Soon the mustang's engine hummed, and Daphne sat in the driver's seat, unable to move. She looked up and noticed the sky was soft and aligned with pink and gold. Another internal struggle ensued.

Her conversation with Renee just two days prior came to mind.

"*I don't expect you to come by every day to see me,*" Renee had said.

"*I know that,*" said Daphne at the time.

"*You have a life, don't you? Go live it.*"

Daphne had been holding onto Renee's hand and trying not to cry. "*It just seems…*"

"*Unfair?*"

"*Exactly.*"

"*Honey, life's not fair. If you keep waiting for it to be fair, you'll wait forever.*"

"*Well, I might not come by on Tuesday night, just so you know.*"

"Then I'll see you on Wednesday or Thursday. Besides, it's not like I'm going anywhere."

The dialogue in Daphne's head could have continued for eternity. Finally, she looked in the mirror and spoke to herself. "Get a grip, Daphne. She's not your mother."

With those words, she began driving toward home.

Chapter 2

After the ACDP meeting, Rachel lingered around the refreshment table. Her stomach growled as she eyeballed the batch of homemade fudge brownies that had been placed in the center. *Surely one couldn't hurt, right?* she thought.

At that moment, Paul, who had just spoken to the group, also approached the table. They both reached for the same brownie simultaneously.

"Oh, I'm sorry!" said Rachel, pulling her hand away.

"No, I insist," Paul said. "Ruth sure makes a mean brownie, doesn't she?"

"I-I wouldn't know. I haven't tried one yet."

"Well then, you're in for a treat."

Rachel took the brownie in one hand and grabbed a napkin with the other. She took her first bite and felt the smooth, velvety chocolate melt in her mouth. "Mmm! That *is* good!"

Just then, an attractive young woman with long, hazelnut hair walked up beside them. She threw a balled-up tissue into a nearby trash can like a basketball. Rachel smiled at her. The woman smiled back. As she turned to leave, the sight of her physique made Rachel regret taking the brownie. "You know," she said, talking to Paul again, "I lost my dad too."

"I'm sorry to hear that. How long has it been?"

Rachel sighed. "Twenty-five years."

Paul shook his head and said, "It never gets easy, does it?"

"No, it doesn't," said Rachel. "I mean, most days I'm so busy with my kids that I almost forget that he's gone. But then on other days it feels like it *just* happened."

"And sometimes you're just going along and something reminds you of him and you start to cry?"

She nodded.

They broke eye contact while Rachel reached for a glass of punch.

"So, you have *kids*," Paul said. "How old are they?"

"Well, I have a daughter who's three and a son who's three months old."

"Holy crap! They must keep you busy!"

"Yes! Avery's a little chatterbox. She just started preschool. Every day she fills me in on her daily activities while we're driving home. Of course, I don't need the report. They have cameras in every room in the building. I can actually use my phone to access pictures anytime. That way, I always know what's going on."

"Boy! Times sure have changed since I had kids. It seems like as soon as they could walk, they'd take off for the day. The only time you saw them was if they were hurt or hungry."

They both laughed.

"Well," said Rachel, "my son Nick isn't even crawling yet but still manages to keep me on my toes."

"Sounds like a lot of work."

"It is. My husband, Lee, is a big help, though. Tuesdays are his day off, so he keeps the kids for me. He even makes dinner, so I get a break. In fact, if it wasn't for him, I probably wouldn't come to these meetings."

"And how long have you been coming?"

"This is my third meeting," she said.

"So…your dad passed decades ago, but you've only been coming for three weeks. What made you start coming *now*?"

Rachel paused. A far-off look spread across her face. "Let's just say, it was overdue."

"Well, better late than never," said Paul.

After that, the two new acquaintances exchanged goodbyes, and Rachel began to walk toward the door. She took her cell phone out of her pocket and texted her husband: "Leaving now. I'll be home in about twenty minutes. How are the kids?"

He answered back: "Kids are fine. We just ate. Feel free to stay out longer if you need to de-stress.

Hmmm, maybe I could try that little Greek diner around the corner. It'd be nice to enjoy a quiet meal by myself.

She texted: "Maybe I will…thanks, baby ☺"

He typed back: "Np ☺"

* * *

When Rachel arrived at the diner, she was greeted by a pretty Albanian hostess, who had just wiped down one of the nearby booths. She looked up as soon as Rachel walked in the door.

"Hi! Can I get you a table?" the hostess asked.

Before Rachel could answer, she noticed the counter lined with barstools. It looked quaint and comfortable, which was perfect for her party of one.

"Actually, I'll just sit at the counter, if that's okay."

"Sure thing," the hostess answered. "Someone will be with you in a minute."

Rachel hoisted herself onto a barstool and sighed. She sat for a moment and listened to the sound of pots clanking and cooks yelling from the kitchen. The counter was so clean that she could see her reflection in it. Her messy bun was lopsided. The contours of her once slender cheeks were now round and pudgy. She frowned.

Don't be so hard on yourself. You just had a baby not long ago.

What was the reason before I got pregnant? And before I got pregnant the first time?

She looked around. The ketchup and mustard bottles on the countertop were placed side by side like a bride and groom on top of a wedding cake. The salt-and-pepper shakers looked the same way. The menus, laid end to end across the counter, appeared to have exactly one foot of space between them, which could not have been by accident.

Someone at the restaurant certainly likes things neat.

Just as Rachel opened her menu, the waitress working the counter approached her. "Can I get you something to drink, ma'am?" she asked in a soft voice.

Rachel looked up to see a young, thin girl with dark brown, almost black, hair. "Just water with lemon, please," she answered.

The waitress nodded and disappeared. Less than thirty seconds later, there was a glass of water in front of Rachel, along with a little saucer filled with lemon wedges.

She's good! Rachel thought.

"Are you ready to order?" asked the waitress. She tucked a strand of her hair behind her ear.

Taking pity on the girl, Rachel tried to engage her in conversation. "What do you recommend?"

The waitress looked up from her notepad for the first time. Her eyes were olive green and quite striking. "Um, well, everything Pete makes is good. But I like his cheeseburgers the best."

"Mmm," said Rachel. "That sounds so good yet so *bad*. I just had a brownie earlier and I wouldn't want to make a pig of myself." She chuckled.

The waitress clenched the pad and pen close to her chest and shrugged.

Rachel closed her menu. "Ah! What the hell, I'll have the cheeseburger, please."

"Coming right up," the waitress said. She scribbled the order on her pad, pulled the ticket off, and handed it to one of the cooks.

Rachel noticed that her waitress was the only person who didn't call out the orders to the kitchen staff. She didn't even yell "Order up!" while hanging the ticket, like the other waitresses. In fact, she barely spoke unless spoken to. It was almost like she was broken inside.

* * *

It was eight o'clock when Rachel arrived at home. The sun was down, and Lee had turned on the porch and foyer lights. When she entered, she took off her shoes and laid them against the wall by the door, beside Lee's work shoes and Avery's little pink sneakers.

Rachel crossed the kitchen on her way to the living room. The air smelled of chicken nuggets and french fries. However, all of the food had been eaten or put away, and all the dishes were done. It was so quiet Rachel could only deduce that her children were both asleep.

In the living room, Lee was asleep on the couch. Avery lay on top of him and snoozed. Each time Lee inhaled and exhaled, his belly rose and fell while Avery's limp little body moved up and down. His head was cocked to the side and his mouth hung open. Avery's little hands rested on her father's shoulders. A tiny puddle of drool had formed on Lee's shirt. It was a precious sight.

Rachel knelt down beside Lee and whispered in his ear, "I'm home."

Lee blinked a few times before his eyes fully opened. He looked down at Avery and beamed with pride.

"Want me to take her to her room?" Rachel asked.

"I don't mind doing it," said Lee. He wrapped his arms around his daughter and sat up. Then he cradled her like a baby and hoisted himself onto his feet.

"Well then," said Rachel. "I'll just hop in the shower and meet you in our room."

"Okay," said Lee. He kissed his wife on the forehead before carrying Avery upstairs.

Moments later, in the master bathroom, Rachel turned on the shower and waited for the water to heat up. As she took her clothes off and stared at herself in the mirror, she was appalled by what she saw. Her thighs seemed to be twice the size they had been when she was younger. She turned to the side and realized that her belly could give others the illusion that she was at least six months pregnant. When she could no longer stand to look at herself, she turned and went into the shower, where she became lost in thought.

Good meeting. Still not sure I'll ever share my story. But if I'm going to keep attending, eventually I may have to… What's the deal with that waitress at the diner? She seems so nice yet so lost. I don't know…Lee really is amazing. The way he takes care of the kids. The way he helps keep the house clean so I don't have to do it all. It makes me feel guilty for what I've put him through, what I still put him through sometimes. I know it's a problem, but how do I stop it?

After she'd showered and dried off, she put on a pair of boxers and an old T-shirt. She came out to find Lee in their bed. The covers were turned down, and the TV was on—all cued up for one of the shows he had recorded for her. His arms were stretched out, which created the perfect resting place on his chest for Rachel to lay her head. She slid into the bed and snuggled close to him, breathing in the comforting scent of his deodorant. Lee kissed her forehead and whispered, "I love you."

She whispered back, "I love you too." *But I don't deserve you.*

Chapter 3

Kate, who had served Rachel earlier that evening, wiped down the counter for the tenth time since the start of her shift. The diner was quiet. All of the customers were gone, except for a few college students who sat across from each other at a booth. They sipped on coffee and checked their social media accounts, ignoring one another. "Do you want me to start closing?" she asked Pete.

"Darling," said Pete, who was the owner and head cook. His term of endearment sounded like *dahr-ling* due to his thick Greek accent. "You *always* close. Go home and rest. You don't look well."

Kate turned and looked at her reflection in the double doors that led to the kitchen. Even though the image was distorted, she could see the dark circles under her eyes. The oversized sleeveless white button-up shirt and black pants she wore made her thin physique even more obvious. "I *am* a little tired," Kate admitted.

"Then go. Go home and rest. Besides, you keep this place so clean there is not much for us to do." He chuckled.

Good ole Pete, Kate thought. "Well, if you're sure."

He kissed her on the cheek. "Yes, darling. Go! We'll see you tomorrow."

Kate blushed and turned away, still unaccustomed to affection. "Good night. I'll see you tomorrow." She dropped her spotless apron into the linen hamper and walked toward the door. Her gaze never left the ground until she was outside.

During her walk home, Kate looked around her. She scanned the opposite side of the street, which was lined with restaurants and antique shops, for unfamiliar faces. Now and then, she turned and glanced over her shoulder to make sure no one was there. Her key, which hung from a Winnie the Pooh keyring, was clasped in her fist. The long edge stuck out between her index and middle fingers.

When she was a couple of blocks from the house that she rented from Pete and his wife, Elizabeth, she thought about the new customer who had come in earlier that evening. Kate could still picture her alone at the counter. Her messy bun and wisps of red hair framed her face, and her smile revealed the tiniest hint of an overbite. She'd made friendly conversation and left a five-dollar tip for a six-dollar cheeseburger.

That was weird! I mean, who does that? Kate thought about it for so long that before she knew it, she was home. The house was a small white bungalow with a green roof. She climbed up the three wooden steps of the front porch and unlocked the door. As soon as she entered, she caught her reflection again, this time in the newly polished wood floor of the foyer. She hung her purse on the hook of a coat rack and then sat on a wooden bench against the opposite wall to remove her shoes. Then she placed them against the wall so she wouldn't dirty the carpet.

Home at last. She yawned. Her stomach growled. The dinner rush had come and gone so suddenly there had been no time to eat. She stepped into the kitchen and opened the refrigerator. There was half of a spinach pie that Elizabeth had made for Sunday dinner, various condiments tucked in the door, cheese slices, diced fruit, and cold cuts. Everything was in its designated spot. After a moment, she grabbed the strawberry preserves from the refrigerator door and retrieved the peanut butter from the pantry. The bread that she kept on top of the refrigerator dropped into her hands with just a tug. She laid everything on the counter and took a knife out of the drawer in front of her. Just before she opened the bag of bread, she felt her cell phone vibrate.

Voicemail? I don't remember it ringing.

Kate pulled the phone out of her pocket and looked at the name on the screen. Her heart began to pound. She bit her lip. *Just play it. It'll drive you crazy if you don't.* She sighed, hit the playback button, and listened.

"Hi, Kate. It's Adam." His voice was one that she both longed to hear and dreaded hearing at the same time. "Um, I'm not really sure why I called. We haven't actually talked since—"

"Don't say it," Kate whispered, as if Adam could hear her. "Don't *say* it."

"Well, you know. Anyway, I've been thinking about you a lot and, um, I hope I hear back from you soon... Okay, bye."

Kate's heart was going hey wire. She closed her eyes and breathed in through her nose.

One... She counted in her head. *Two. Three. Four.*

Then she exhaled through her nose.

One...two...three...four... Don't play it again. Just delete it.

Her stomach, which had growled moments before, was now in knots.

She held her index finger up to the number 7, which would delete Adam's message. However, she couldn't bring herself to follow through. Instead, she turned the phone off and pushed it away.

Staring at the food spread on the counter, Kate realized she'd lost her appetite. She didn't sleep a wink that night.

Chapter 4

The next morning, Daphne's alarm chimed at five o'clock. She had been lying on her stomach. The rude noise made her head jolt upward. She pulled her hand out from under the covers and tapped the phone multiple times, trying to hit the "dismiss" button, to no avail. Finally, the phone fell to the floor, disengaging the alarm. *Ugh!* she groaned.

Come on, Daphne. She argued with herself. *Get your ass out of bed.*

I'm sooo tired.

If you don't get up now, you won't be able to work out again until tomorrow...unless you bail on Renee again.

Not an option.

What's it going to be then? You need to burn off the Chinese food you ate last night!

Daphne kicked the covers off and rolled out of bed. She left the bed unmade and stumbled to the other side of her bedroom to the dresser. It took a few minutes to open each drawer and find the right combination of spandex pants, sports bra, and tank top. By the time she'd picked out a pair of socks, she had no patience left to close the top drawer.

After getting dressed, Daphne ambled to the vanity. On the way, she nearly tripped over a pair of pants she'd left on the floor the previous night, which had missed the hamper by mere inches. She turned the light on and revealed the cluttered countertop—hair accessories, toothpaste, and makeup were sprawled everywhere. The round hairbrush she'd been looking for caught her eye, and she used it to detangle and set her hair into a ponytail. When she was done, she surveyed herself in the mirror from top to bottom.

To the untrained eye, Daphne had a well-toned figure. However, she could not see past her flaws.

God, my butt looks huge! Will this muffin top ever completely go away? Ugh! How about this pooch? I can't look anymore.

She reached under the sink for the mouthwash and took a swig. After she'd swished and gargled long enough to get the stale taste out of her mouth, she spat out the rinse, turned off the light, and walked to the kitchen. The light that crept in from the street outside allowed her to see where she was going. As she passed by the kitchen sink, she noticed the dishes were still piled up from the day before. She ignored them and grabbed a bottle of water from the refrigerator.

At that point, Daphne walked to the entryway and turned on the light. Half of her shoe collection lay on the floor in disarray. Her sneakers were lying in two separate spots. She grabbed them both, sat on the floor, and slipped them on without untying or retying the laces. After that, she grabbed the keys off the baker's rack on the wall that faced the door. With her keys, water, and phone in hand, Daphne left for the gym.

* * *

Later that afternoon, upon arrival at the hospital, Daphne noticed her preferred spot was available.

Phew! Now I don't have to go through the emergency department.

Inside the building, it felt about twenty degrees cooler. The air smelled of hospital disinfectant, making the inside of her nose tingle. Her sneakers squeaked across the freshly waxed floor. The noise echoed down the hallway. It made her recall a time she was taking a walk with Renee around the oncology wing.

"There is something magical about hospitals, don't you think?" Renee had said.

"What do you mean?" Daphne had asked.

"Think about it. Within these walls, babies are being born. People are dying. People who were dying make miraculous recoveries. Sometimes

even babies that were just born or were about to be born suddenly pass away. If somebody wants to see God's work, they just need to come to a hospital."

Presently, Daphne rounded the corner and saw the sign for the hospital chapel. The irony made her smile.

Once she passed the chapel, she smelled the comforting aroma of vegetable soup. Her mouth watered. She almost turned toward the cafeteria instead of the elevators.

Nah. Better wait and see if Renee wants to eat with me. With any luck, she'll say yes to something besides popsicles today.

The elevator was just ahead now, and the doors were open. Daphne quickly ran up to catch it. The woman inside saw Daphne and held her hand out so the doors wouldn't close on her.

"Thanks," Daphne said as she stepped inside.

"No problem," said the woman. She appeared to be in her early thirties and had dark blond hair pulled back in a ponytail. She wore a pink T-shirt and sweatpants and had dark circles under her eyes. "What floor?" she asked.

"Four, please," said Daphne. "Thanks."

"So are you visiting someone?" the woman asked.

For a moment, Daphne froze, unsure of how to answer.

Relax. She didn't ask who you're visiting. Stop being a baby and answer the question.

"Um, yes. How about you?"

"My husband," she nodded. "He just got out of surgery a few days ago. Last night was the first night I slept in my own bed since he was admitted. But I came back as soon as I got up and ready this morning."

"That's so nice. You must love him a lot."

"I do," she said with dreamy eyes.

The elevator came to a halt on the fourth floor, and the doors flew open.

"Well," Daphne said before stepping out. "I hope you're able to take him home soon."

"Thank you. And good luck to you."

"Thanks," Daphne called just before the elevator doors came to a full close.

She stared at her reflection in the elevator doors. The silence was deafening.

You should have told her whom you're here to see. What the hell is wrong with you?

When Daphne got to the room, Renee was watching TV. Her head was turned away from the door, and the light from the TV outlined her profile. Her cheekbones and clavicle protruded, although not nearly as badly as they had a few months prior. The color in her cheeks had also improved. Her sandy blond hair was starting to grow back. There was about two inches all around now. She had a peaceful smile on her delicate face.

Daphne could feel the tears welling up. *Stop it! Or Renee will cry too.* She cleared her throat. "Hey!"

Renee's head turned. Her smile grew. "Hey yourself." She reached up.

Daphne leaned in and they hugged. "How are you feeling today?"

"Uh…," Renee hesitated. She looked away briefly and then back at Daphne again. "You know, I've gotten so used to trying not to think about the pain that sometimes I don't realize how I feel until somebody asks me."

"Oh, sorry," she said, feeling stupid. "I guess maybe I shouldn't have asked."

"No, no, it's okay. I actually feel pretty good," she said. "My nausea is almost totally gone. I'm staying awake more. I think I might be ready for a little exercise."

"Do you want to take a walk around the hallways?"

"You talked me into it," said Renee. She pushed the covers off.

"Do we need to call the nurse or anything?

"Nah. I'm not hooked up to anything right now."

Daphne was stunned. Like Renee, who'd gotten used to ignoring her pain, Daphne had gotten used to ignoring the machines and tubes. She now realized they weren't there. *Am I actually seeing this right now?*

Renee did, however, need Daphne's arm to hoist herself up from the bed. Once she was standing, they made sure her gown was securely tied in the back. Then they started walking toward the door slowly but steadily, arm in arm.

"You know," said Daphne once they entered the hallway, "I could probably bring you some of your clothes the next time I come."

Renee smiled weakly. "Well, that'd be great. Just make sure it's something I can slip on and off easily."

"Are they still running a million tests on you every day?" Daphne sounded irritated.

"Not *every* day. On and off, really. It depends on how strong I feel. They don't want to slow down my recovery just because they're trying to stay one step ahead of this thing."

They got to the first corner and turned right.

Daphne was surprised by Renee's comment. "Why do they? I mean—"

"I'm sure they're just trying to be cautious, sweetie. Don't worry. I think the worst of it is over."

"Yeah, I hope so."

They walked in silence for a few minutes until Daphne broke it.

"So I've been recording 'Tomorrow Always Comes.' Have you been watching?"

"Oh my gosh! That Susan is such a *liar*."

"I know! I can't *stand* her!"

"Mark my words, the truth is going to come out and bite her in the ass one of these days!"

They laughed and carried on like teenage girls about their silly daytime drama. Some onlookers shook their heads as they passed, while others smiled with delight. Daphne tried not to care but couldn't help wondering if they were being judged.

Before they knew it, they'd been walking for over twenty minutes, and Renee started getting tired.

"Did you want to go a little farther?" Daphne asked, trying to encourage her. "Maybe grab some dinner in the cafeteria?"

Renee sighed deeply. "Actually, can you bring me back something, sweetie? I think I may have overdone it."

22

Daphne could feel Renee's body getting a little heavier as her strength wore off. She scanned the area and noticed a nurse's station nearby, which had a walker leaning against the edge.

"Excuse me," Daphne said to the nurse standing there. "Do you think we could borrow that walker for a few minutes?"

The nurse was an African American woman with short curly hair. She wore blue scrubs adorned with baby elephants. As soon as the nurse looked at Renee, it was clear that they'd met. "For Nene?" she said in a sassy voice. "You got it, honey!"

Renee rolled her eyes like a child who'd just been embarrassed by her parent. "Hello, Pearl," she said, unable to contain her amusement.

Pearl looked right at Daphne. "And you must be the daughter she's always talking about…Daphne?"

Now Daphne was the one who was embarrassed. *Ugh! It'll break Renee's heart if I correct her.* "Yes, I'm Daphne." She extended her hand.

Pearl shook her hand firmly. "Nice to meet you, darlin.' I can take it from here. Why don't you run down and grab yourself a little supper? You look like you could use a hot meal." She came around to the front of the nurse's station and slid the walker in front of Renee. Renee let go of Daphne's arm, one hand at a time, and leaned on the walker. Everything seemed under control.

"Well, I'm okay. But I think I'm going to grab something for Renee."

"Whatchu want, Nene?" Pearl asked.

"A bagel would be great," said Renee. "With cream cheese." She slid the walker forward. Pearl was right beside her, keeping watch.

"You got it," Daphne said as she started walking toward the elevator.

All the way down to the cafeteria, her thoughts tortured her.

Why were you so uncomfortable when the woman in this elevator earlier asked you if you were visiting someone? And why did you answer Pearl that way?

The elevator ride, like her internal dialogue, seemed perpetual.

Finally, the doors opened, and she walked off the elevator and over to the cafeteria. She stood in line and scanned the selection, hoping something would appeal to her, but nothing did. When it was her turn, she ordered Renee's bagel, paid, and stepped to the side. While she waited, she looked around at the other people sitting at the white and silver tables, enjoying their meals. *I wonder if any of them are here to see their mothers.*

"Here's your bagel!" the cashier announced suddenly. "Have a good evening!"

"Thank you," Daphne said, grabbing the plated bagel.

By the time she got back to the room, Renee had fallen asleep.

Daphne placed the bagel on the bedside table and covered it with a napkin. Before leaving, she leaned in and kissed Renee softly on her temple. *I'm sorry, Renee… I'm so sorry.*

Chapter 5

The following Tuesday, Rachel walked into the gymnasium with a lump in her throat. Her heart felt like it had dropped into her stomach. She stopped at the entrance and took a deep breath before walking in.

On the outside, she looked remarkable. Her hair was flat-ironed so that the bottom rested perfectly on her shoulders, while the top layers framed her face. There was a piece of bang that lay on her forehead, almost covering one eye. Makeup had been applied as well. She wore a gray sweater with three-quarter sleeves, a pair of black dress pants, and boots with one-inch heels. To complete her look, Rachel had adorned herself with a necklace, earrings, watch, and bracelet—all of which had been gifts from Lee.

After Opening Dedication, updates, and one new story, the floor remained open. Ruth, who was leading the meeting again, asked for the second time if there was anyone else who wanted to share. Everyone sat in awkward silence.

Now or never, Rachel thought. She stood up.

"Hi, what's your name?" Ruth asked excitedly.

She gulped. "My name is Rachel."

"Hi, Rachel," said the audience.

"Well, thank you for standing up, Rachel," said Ruth, gesturing toward the stage. "Please, won't you?"

Everyone clapped as she walked to the stage, up the stairs, and stood behind the podium. The last speaker had been much taller than Rachel, so Ruth had to walk over and lower the microphone for her. Rachel could feel her cheeks getting red, but it didn't stop her.

She almost stopped, however, after she looked out among the crowd for the first time and saw all of the faces staring back at her.

Instantly, she summoned the words of wisdom given by her Speech professor during her freshman year of college. Rachel could picture her vividly standing before the class. Her white hair was in a bun. She wore a denim vest over a white T-shirt and a maxi skirt. A peace symbol medallion dangled from her neck. She looked like the personification of Mother Earth. On the first day of class, she had said, "Look at these faces. These people are your support system. These are your friends. And *nobody* in this group wants to see you fall flat on your face."

Rachel smiled. She was finally ready.

"So," Ruth said, "when did you lose a parent?"

Rachel took another deep breath. Her heart was thumping like a jackrabbit. "When I was seven," she began. "My father—" Her chest tightened. Sweat began to form under her arms.

"It's okay, Rachel," said Ruth. "You can take your time. Why don't you just tell us a little bit about him?"

Rachel sighed. "He was a great dad. He was funny and always made me feel special. He used to tuck me in at night and read to me. He loved singing to me too...on the nights he wasn't working late, I mean."

"What did he do?" Ruth asked.

"He owned a jewelry store... One night, it was time to close the shop, and a man came in. My dad thought he was a customer. He tried to tell the man that the store was closed...and...the man pulled out a gun."

Some members of the audience gasped. A few put their hands on their faces in disbelief.

"My father begged for his life. He even offered to let the man take whatever jewelry he wanted if he would just let him go." Rachel's hands shook. "But the guy shot him anyway. He managed to break some glass and grab about ten thousand dollars' worth of jewelry before he took off." Her voice began to crack. "He ran into the woods behind the store. The police caught him about two miles away and arrested him. He went to trial, was found guilty, and now he's in prison."

"Rachel," asked Ruth in a soft voice. "Does it comfort you to know that justice was served for you father?"

Rachel wiped a tear from her eye. "A little." She nodded. "But it still hurts. He never got to meet his grandkids, and they'll never know him. Plus…" She stopped herself before she said too much. "Nothing has been the same since he passed, especially between me and my mom."

"Well, Rachel, I think it took a lot of guts for you to share this story."

The audience burst into applause. It took all of Rachel's strength not to sob and throw herself onto the podium. She held on to the edges firmly and breathed deeply until the noise subsided.

"And let me tell you from the bottom of my heart," said Ruth, "I am so, *so* sorry for your loss. I hope this will be a first step toward healing for you because you deserve it."

More applause followed.

Ruth reached out to give Rachel a hug. Rachel hesitated at first but slowly leaned in. She let Ruth hold her for a moment, and she cried quietly on her shoulder. Ruth patted her back and whispered, "It's okay, sweetie. It's okay." It was the first time in years that someone had hugged Rachel like that—the way a mother hugs a child. Even though it was brief, she realized then it was something she'd been missing.

After the meeting, Rachel found herself at the refreshment table again. It was the same cheerful spread as the week before: tiny bottles of water, punch, diced fruit, cheese and crackers, chocolate chip cookies, and (of course) Ruth's brownies. Rachel had just picked up a brownie when she heard a man's voice. "I *told* you they were good."

Startled, she turned and looked at the speaker. "Hi, Paul," she said.

Paul opened his arms to hug her. Once again, she gave in.

"I'm really proud of you for standing up there tonight," said Paul.

"Oh, thanks." Her cheeks began to blush. "Could you tell I was terrified?"

"Nah, cool as a cucumber." He chuckled.

"Excuse me," another voice intervened. This time, it was a female voice. Rachel and Paul looked over and saw a woman who was about Rachel's age, but she was more slender with hazelnut hair. "You're Rachel, right?"

"Yeah, that's me," said Rachel, who was caught off guard.

"I just wanted to introduce myself. My name's Daphne." She extended her hand, and Rachel shook it.

Daphne and Paul also shook hands.

"Nice to meet you," Daphne said.

"A pleasure," said Paul.

Daphne's glance returned to Rachel. "I just wanted to tell you how much you inspired me tonight. I mean, your story is *incredible*, and it took a lot of guts to share it!"

"Well, thanks," said Rachel.

The three of them made small talk for a few minutes. It was clear that they were going to get along. Before they parted ways that night, Paul suggested that whoever arrived first the following week should save seats for the other two.

Rachel and Daphne happily agreed.

Chapter 6

The next morning, Kate was sitting at the medical clinic downtown. Pete had dropped her off early, before he had to open the restaurant. After more than a week with no signs of improvement, he insisted that she go get checked out.

As she sat on the paper-covered examining table, her stomach growled. They had asked her to fast overnight so they could do a full blood screening. Her hunger was so intense now that she felt nauseated. *How long can they keep me waiting?*

The day had already been unpleasant.

Upon arrival, Kate had been greeted by a less-than-friendly receptionist.

"What brings you in today?" she had asked, barely making eye contact.

"Well, I've been feeling really tired for the last couple of weeks and I just don't feel like myself."

The receptionist glared at Kate from behind her designer glasses, which she adjusted with the tip of her middle finger. She said nothing. Then to make matters worse, the paperwork that she handed Kate looked as thick as a Bible.

Kate sat down and filled out what she could. Over and over, she rolled her eyes when she came upon a question about family history. *How can you know your family history when you don't have a family?*

When she was done, she handed the paperwork to the rude receptionist and hoped that the unanswered questions wouldn't be a problem. Luckily, she wasn't spoken to again until a few minutes later when her name was called.

"Kate Jones," the young male nurse said, standing in the doorway with a clipboard in his hand. She followed him into the hallway where he checked her height, weight, temperature, and blood pressure. After that, she sat in a small chair next to the scale while he reviewed the questions from her paperwork quietly to himself.

"So what seems to be the problem today?"

Do I really have to answer that question again?

She repeated the answer she'd given the receptionist.

Again she was given a strange look. This time, however, it didn't seem to be filled with disdain. "That sounds pretty general," said the nurse.

"Sorry," Kate said.

"Well, it could be a simple nutritional deficiency. From your questionnaire, it looks like you don't take multivitamins."

"Guilty." She smiled crookedly.

He scanned her paperwork again. "And you're twenty-seven…"

"Uh-huh." She nodded.

"That's probably it. The doctor will be able to tell you for sure."

* * *

The doctor's examining room was still empty, except for Kate. Her stomach growled again. She found herself scanning the room for a place to vomit—if it came to that. *What could be taking so long?*

She imagined what Pete would say if he'd been sitting there with her now. *"When you have to wait on an answer, the answer is worth waiting for,"* he would say.

"We'll see," Kate whispered to herself.

Finally, there was a knock on the door.

"Hello," the doctor said, walking in. She was in her mid-forties with blond, shoulder-length hair, and blue eyes. Her pristine white coat looked like it had just been bleached and pressed, and the shiny glare from the stethoscope cast a fleeting beam of light as she closed the door behind her. "I'm Doctor Bishop and you're…Kate?"

"Yeah. It's nice to meet you." Kate shook her hand weakly.

"Likewise." The doctor sat down across from Kate and opened her file. For a moment, she didn't say a word. Kate began to worry. She braced herself. The doctor sighed and looked up at Kate.

"Okay, so your blood pressure is a little low, but nothing to be concerned about. So that's good. Your weight and height are normal, of course. Your temperature is fine too."

Why are you telling me what's right with me? Tell me what's wrong. "So," Kate asked, "what about the blood screenings? Is it, like, low *iron*? Is it *diabetes*?"

"No"—the doctor shook her head—"nothing like that. You're *fine.*"

Kate felt both relieved and frustrated. But before she could ask for clarification, the doctor stood up and put her hand on Kate's shoulder, looking quite serious. "I do, however, want you to follow up with your regular doctor. The sooner the better."

"Why?" asked Kate, whose eyes had widened.

The doctor leaned in and answered, "You're pregnant."

Chapter 7

It was Friday afternoon the following week. Daphne was at work, looking forward to a restful weekend. The night before, she'd gone to the hospital again. Now that Renee seemed to be improving, it had taken some of the pressure off Daphne to visit so often. Plus, the nurses and doctors had been taking such good care of Renee that she didn't seem to want for anything.

She was typing away at her keyboard when the phone rang.

"Simon and Associates," she said into the phone. "This is Daphne. How may I help you?"

"Hi, Daphne, this is Allison from Ryan Dunovan's office," said the perky voice on the other end.

Daphne's heart stopped. She was expecting the call but not so soon.

"Oh, hi!" she responded, trying to sound excited.

"Sorry to interrupt you at work. I tried calling your cell phone, but it went straight to voicemail."

"Oh, no problem."

"Anyway, I was calling to follow up with you about the inquiry that you recently submitted. Is this a good time to talk?"

Daphne quickly looked around to make sure no one was eavesdropping. "Uh…yes, ma'am. This is fine."

"Great! So these things tend to move sort of backward. There's some information I need to confirm with you before we get started. But first, I need to be absolutely certain that you have no reservations about starting this… Sometimes the outcome is not what the client hopes for, and it can be pretty devastating."

"I understand," said Daphne, who already expected the worst anyway.

"Okay. Second, we need to ensure that the information you give us is completely accurate to the best of your knowledge."

To the best of my knowledge... "I'll tell you everything I can. I promise."

"So you want to go ahead and move forward, is that right?"

Daphne said nothing. She bit her lip and shook her head.

"Are you still there?" Allison asked.

"Yes, I'm here," she answered. "And yes, I definitely want to move forward." *Ugh! I'm an idiot!*

"Okay." Allison chuckled in relief. "So we have the adoption date as May 5, 1980. Is that right?"

"Yes, ma'am," said Daphne.

"Do you know what state you were born in?"

Daphne's heart stopped again. "I...don't know."

There was a brief pause on the other end. "Okay. Do you think you could find out for us? It would really help us out."

"I'll try," Daphne said. *Not sure how, but I'll try.*

"Great! And the adoptive mother, Renee Weavers. What's *her* date of birth?"

"November 18, 1958."

"Okay, and where was Renee living in 1980?"

Ugh! Ask me something I know the answer to. "Actually, I'm not sure."

There was a pregnant pause. "What about Renee's husband, is he still alive?"

Oh, this just keeps getting better. "He is alive, but they're divorced."

"Oh, I'm sorry to hear that. By any chance, do you know the year that they were married?"

Daphne began thinking out loud, "Um, I remember her telling me that she and Brock had been married for three full years before the adoption...and their anniversary was in December, so best I can figure...December 1976?"

"Okay, great!" Allison was starting to sound encouraged. "Now what about where Renee was born?"

"Tuscon, Arizona," Daphne answered instantly. That was something she could never forget.

"Okay," said Allison. "I think we definitely have enough information to get things started."

"How long does it usually take?"

Allison sighed deeply. "Well, it depends. Best case scenario, a few weeks. Worst case, a few months. Some cases have taken close to a year."

"Wow, really?" said Daphne.

"Yeah, unfortunately, even when we have leads, some turn up as dead ends. Sometimes records are lost or changed. The other people involved sometimes relocate, making it harder to find them, or they've passed on. Sometimes we get a hit on a lead, but the person on the other end is dishonest or unwilling to talk to us. A person can change their number to one that's unlisted. Basically, some people don't want to be found."

What am I doing? "Well, thank you for your honesty, Allison. I appreciate it."

"You're welcome, Daphne. Thank you for the information. I'm hoping this will turn out well. And please call us if you find out any information that could help."

"Okay, I will."

"Have a great day. I'll keep you posted on whatever we find."

"You too. And thanks. Bye."

"Bye."

As Daphne hung up the phone, a feeling of dread brewed in her stomach. *There's no other way.* She took a deep breath, grabbed her cell phone, and started dialing.

Chapter 8

L ee pulled his Cadillac SUV into the wrap around driveway at home and stopped just a few feet from the garage. He was relieved when he turned off the engine and no longer had to endure the sounds of the "Wheels on the Bus" Pandora station. Avery, on the other hand, was still jabbering about her day at pre-school. As her daddy, he offered the obligatory "Really?" and "You did?" often enough to let his daughter know he was listening.

When Lee got out of the car, he moved around to the back to unbuckle Avery from her car seat. He then walked her by the hand to the first stone in a path that led up to their front door. The task of stepping from one stone to the next would occupy her mind long enough for him to get Nick.

"To the door, Avery!" Lee called happily. "Let's say our ABCs...A—"

"B!" shouted Avery, stepping onto the second stone.

Lee double-checked for cars moving about the neighborhood. The streets were clear, and it was quiet. "C!" he called while he unstrapped Nick.

"D!" Avery yelled, now on the fourth stone.

"E!" Lee placed his son on his left hip and grabbed a takeout bag from the back seat floor. He peeked around the car to make sure Avery was still standing before shutting the car door.

"F!" said Avery, who now stood at the front door.

They continued their game while Lee locked the car and approached the house. Since Avery had run out of stones to step on, she bounced on the welcome mat with each new letter. Lee unlocked the door while balancing his infant son and the family's dinner at the same time.

"N!" called Avery as the door opened.

"O!" said Lee, who'd almost forgotten they were playing. He could still hear Avery's voice as he stepped into the foyer. His mind, however, became fixated on the image before him. Rachel's purse and shoes were thrown carelessly at the bottom of the stairs. He scanned upward and saw articles of clothing lying intermittently on multiple steps, like a *Hansel and Gretel* trail of breadcrumbs. He listened close and heard the shower running.

He sighed. *Not again.*

"Daddy, you didn't say Q," Avery said.

"Hey, Avery?" said Lee, changing the subject. "Let's go into the living room and you can play in your play yard while I check on Mommy."

"Okay, Daddy," she agreed and followed him into the living room on her tiptoes.

As quickly as he could, Lee placed the food on the floor and secured his son in his baby swing. He pressed the button for the lowest setting. Instrumental Beethoven music played instantly, and Nick wiggled his hands and feet with delight. Then Lee turned to Avery, scooped her up, and placed her inside the plastic enclosure they had set up for when they needed to step out of the room without her. She took a few steps away and opened her toy box.

"I'll be right back, sweetie," he said and he headed for the stairs.

Avery waved but said nothing. She was focused on her baby doll, who was clearly in need of a pretend bottle.

Lee stood at the bottom of the stairs and looked up. He prepared himself for the worst.

As he climbed each step, the sound of the shower grew louder and louder. He opened the bedroom door slowly and stuck his head inside. Nothing seemed out of place. All he could hear was the shower.

Lee walked in and removed his shoes, using his feet to slide them against the wall near the door. He took off his watch and laid it on top of the dresser. Taking a deep breath, he sauntered to the bathroom door. He knocked gently.

"Rachel, it's Lee. Can I come in!" he called.

There was no answer.

"Rachel?" he called a little louder.

Still nothing.

"I'm coming in!" he yelled.

When he opened the door, the steam from the shower started pouring out. The mirror was completely fogged. He stepped in and turned toward the shower. His heart sank. There was his wife—huddled on the shower floor in a fetal position. The hot water had made her skin beet-red, yet she shook. She held a washcloth between her legs and rocked slowly back and forth.

Not again... At first, Lee knelt down and tapped the glass, trying not to startle her. He failed. The sound made her jump. She gasped and turned to see who was there.

"It's okay," he said, making eye contact. "It's okay. It's me."

Like a coma patient who had just awakened, she looked around and realized what was happening. "Lee?"

"Yeah, babe. Are you okay? Will you come out?"

Rachel turned away from her husband and sobbed.

Lee could see he had no choice. He grabbed a towel from a nearby rack and opened the shower door. Fully clothed, he stepped in and turned off the water. Getting eye level with Rachel, he wrapped the towel around her. He held her shoulders and waited. "Sweetie?" he said.

Rachel finally looked at him.

"Hey." He smiled bravely.

She leaned in and allowed him to embrace her. Lee held her as tight as he could. His pants and socks were soaked. The heat coming from Rachel's body coupled with the steam made him sweat, but he didn't care.

"I love you," he whispered.

This only made Rachel cry more. "Why?"

"Because you're *you*." His answer was always the same.

Rachel pulled away and shook her head. "I don't get that."

"That's because you can't see what I see. I see past *this*. You're strong. You're an amazing mother. You love me and take care of me..."

"I'm damaged!" she said.

"You're not damaged," Lee corrected her. "You've just been through a lot. It'll be okay. You've just had a setback. We move forward, right?"

Rachel looked at him like a scared child, the way she had countless times when he said those same words to her.

Lee held her again and placed his hand on her head. Neither one of them said a word.

Chapter 9

I t had been weeks since Kate learned she was pregnant and she hadn't told anyone. When Pete and Elizabeth asked about her doctor's visit, she only said that she was advised to start taking vitamin supplements (which was true, after all). It seemed to be enough to satisfy them, and Kate returned to work. She had yet to follow up with her gynecologist. As for the baby's father, that was another story entirely.

One Tuesday Kate ended her shift at the restaurant earlier than usual and set off on a different route. As she walked the mile to her destination, her thoughts were on her birth parents—the ones she couldn't remember but couldn't forget about. *What were they like? What kind of parent would I make? I wish I had a mom to talk to. How can I be a mother if I don't remember my mother? What am I going to do?*

She arrived at the community center just after four o'clock. The gymnasium was full of folding chairs arranged into neat rows, leaving room for a wide aisle down the middle. There was no one else there, except for two ladies, who were facing each other and talking in front of a sign-in table. One of them was wearing a sticker with the name Ruth. As soon as she saw Kate enter, she excused herself and walked toward her.

"Hi!" Ruth said. "Can I help you?"

"Hi," Kate said, looking up just long enough to make eye contact and then dropping her glance again. "Um, I came for the meeting at four thirty...ACDP? I know I'm a little early—"

"That's okay, honey," said Ruth. "We're glad you came." She clasped her hands, almost as if praying. "Feel free to sit and relax. I need to go set up."

"Can I help?" Kate offered.

"Oh, no, no, sweetheart. You just make yourself comfortable, and I'll take care of everything. Other people should be arriving soon."

"All right," said Kate, who then sat in one of the back rows and waited. She remained silent and watched the rest of the attendees come in. Any looks or salutations that she wasn't able to avoid were met with a brave half smile and a nod. She slouched in her seat, trying not to be noticed.

Now and then Kate's eyes scanned the gymnasium. Most of her attention was on Ruth, who had wheeled in a shelved cart to set up a refreshment table. First, Ruth laid out a long red plastic tablecloth. Then she tugged and checked about four times to make sure it was even on all sides. Kate wasn't totally convinced it was even when Ruth stopped, but she said nothing. She continued to observe as Ruth unloaded the rest of the items: two pitchers of punch, plastic cups, paper napkins, a vegetable tray, some cut-up fruit with dip, and about two dozen homemade brownies. Kate's stomach growled loudly. *I hope nobody heard that.*

A little later, in another section of the gymnasium, she saw a man who was probably in his seventies talking to a younger woman. Kate hadn't been trying to eavesdrop on their conversation, but somehow she couldn't help herself.

"Hey, Paul!" The woman said.

"Hey, Daphne! How are you?" the man responded.

The woman looked at her watch. "So I know you've been coming for a while. Do these meetings always start late?"

Kate looked at her watch out of curiosity. It was four thirty on the nose.

Paul chuckled. "Young lady, there ain't no such thing as 'late.' Things happen when they're supposed to happen. Not a moment too late or too soon."

A pensive look came over the woman's face. "Guess I never thought of it that way."

"Well, when you get to be a little older and wiser, you don't worry about those kinds of things. People have become slaves to things like start times, deadlines, and things like that. People need to learn to let go. I mean, we can't control *everything*, right?"

"That's certainly true," she answered.

"Have you seen Rachel?" asked the gentleman.

They both looked around.

"Actually, no," the woman replied.

"Hmm. Maybe she'll sneak in after the meeting starts."

The two sat down side by side.

Kate looked at the stage. A handsome, middle-aged man with salt-and-pepper hair and glasses walked up the steps to the stage. He was wearing tan pants, a green polo shirt, and a plaid blazer. His loafers shuffled softly as he sauntered to the podium. He adjusted the microphone and his glasses before taking a folded note out of his lapel pocket.

"Good afternoon," he said, unfolding the note and laying it on top of the podium.

"Ah, for those of you who don't know me, I'm Ray."

"Hi, Ray," said the audience.

"Also, for those who don't know me, I'm a professor of world religions at the community college. Today, I want to talk a little bit about silence. Silence is underrated. The first time I think I really tapped into silence was when my mother died…before my eyes. I saw the life literally leave her body, like an invisible bird taking flight. And what was left was just the physical body that she had once occupied."

Kate looked around. A few people shifted in their seats, perhaps uncomfortable with the subject matter. She looked at Ray again.

"And in that moment," said Ray, "it got quiet…*so* quiet. See, we don't realize how much noise we've become accustomed to. We're often listening to things on our devices, or we're in conversation with other people, or listening to music when we're driving. And then we come home and turn on our TVs and run our appliances and

41

take showers, which create noise. The list goes on and on. These noises are like layers of an onion." His hands began to move in conjunction with his analogy. His eyes scanned the faces in the group. "Let's say you peeled back a layer. You turn off the TV, the music, the appliances. You'd probably hear the hum of the air conditioner, if it's running. Or you may hear a soft, continuous ringing. And if you peel back another layer, you might start tuning in to things that you've never noticed before, like birds chirping, for example." He took another pause. This one was longer. "Then if you peel back the last layer..." His eyes stopped on Kate.

Her eyes were locked on him, like she couldn't look away...like his words were for *her* ears.

"That bottom core layer," said Ray, "that's *real* silence...and *that silence* is where we find *the truth*."

Chapter 10

Daphne was sitting at a coffee house with a tall white chocolate mocha with almond milk and a warm croissant. Her fingers tapped the table nervously as she checked her social media account for the fourth time. *What's taking him so long? I'll bet he's not coming.* She took another sip of her coffee and took the last bite of her croissant. The butter and pastry flakes had caked onto her fingertips.

She fumbled through her purse for a pouch of wet wipes, cleaned her hands, and then wadded up the wipe, dropping it on the table with the rest of her trash. Just before reaching for her cell phone, she heard a man's voice.

"Hey, Daphne."

Daphne recognized his Southern drawl. She looked up. Her pulse quickened. "Hello, Brock," she answered without getting up from her seat.

"How have you been?" asked Brock.

"Fine," she said, emotionless and to the point. "How are you?"

"Okay, I guess," he answered. "Just workin' and stuff."

The two stared at each other for a moment.

"This is weird," said Brock. "I don't know if I should hug you or sit down or what."

"I think we're past the hugging stage," Daphne said, taking another sip.

Brock bowed his head. His shoulders stooped.

"I just have a couple of questions for you."

"Daphne," he said as he sat down, "I've been trying to figure out a way to say something to you…for a really long time."

She swallowed, trying to suppress the lump in her throat. "Just…say it, I guess."

"I'm really sorry… I'm sorry things didn't work out between me and your mom. I'm sorry I wasn't around more. I took a job offer that I couldn't refuse. I figured if I couldn't see you every day, at least I could support you guys financially."

Daphne fought back the tears. She took a deep breath and looked away. *Don't let him see you cry.* "Well, that's not why I called you." Her head turned to face him again. "I really need some information."

"Okay," he said, clearing his throat. His eyes drooped like a sad puppy. "What can I help you with?"

"I'm looking for some information about my adoption. I really need to know which state I was born in."

"So you're doing it, aren't you? You're trying to find your birth mom?"

Daphne sighed. "Yes."

"Just curious, why not ask Renee that question?"

"Let's just say, I don't want to upset her right now."

"Why would she be upset that you want to know where you came from?"

Daphne said nothing.

"Is she okay?"

"Yes," she lied. "Renee is fine. There's just a lot going on right now, and I don't want to add anything else to her plate."

"Okay," said Brock, hesitating. "The truth is…"

"What?" she asked impatiently. *Why is he being so weird about this?*

"The truth is, I don't know."

Daphne's heart dropped into her stomach. "What do you mean you don't know?"

"I mean your mom and I were already on a waiting list with an adoption agency. Things were on track for us to adopt within the year. We were taking parenting classes and everything."

Too bad you didn't learn from them.

"Then one day, your mom got a phone call from a friend in Tucson that she used to go to school with. She was a sister in the convent there. And this friend told her that a baby had been dropped off at her church—the one they attended when they were kids. There was no birth certificate. Just *you*."

Daphne sat with her jaw open.

"We were living in New Mexico by then, and she asked us if we would consider adopting you. So we packed a bag and caught the next flight to Tucson. And as soon as we laid eyes on you, that was it."

"So I was born in Tucson."

"I'm saying, we *found* you in Tucson. You could have come from *anywhere*."

"What do you mean?" Daphne said, growing increasingly frustrated.

"Think about it. If somebody wanted to abandon a child at a church and there was no birth certificate, clearly they wouldn't want to leave a trail. Someone could have crossed state lines so they wouldn't be found. You could've been born in Colorado or Nevada for all we know."

"Well, you *are* the expert on abandoning children, aren't you?"

Brock's cheeks reddened like a bull. "Daphne! I'm tired of being blamed for everything that went wrong! You've never been married. You don't know how complicated it can get. Now I'll take the blame for the first few years after the divorce, but after you became an adult, you could've reached out. You could've answered the e-mails I sent, but you didn't. *You* wrote *me* off!"

Daphne suddenly realized how ugly she'd been. "I'm sorry… This just isn't what I wanted to hear."

"I'm sorry too," he said. "But you asked me, and I wanted to tell you the truth."

She nodded. "Got it." Then she started to get up from her chair.

"Wait a minute." He grabbed her arm gently.

Startled, she froze. "What?"

He had his eyes closed tightly, as if he was trying to remember something. "Sister Angelina."

Daphne looked puzzled.

"That was the name of Renee's friend in the convent," he went on. "I can't remember the name of the church, but her name was *definitely* Sister Angelina."

"Well, thanks, I guess. But what's an investigator supposed to do with *that*?"

"Maybe you need to do your own investigating," he said.

She didn't want to admit it, but Brock was probably right.

Chapter 11

"Your mom called last night," Lee told Rachel. They were sitting across from each other at their kitchen table. Avery, who had just finished a bowl of Fruit Loops, was watching *Sesame Street* in the living room. Nick was finally asleep after being restless and inconsolable overnight. Afterward, Rachel had been unable to fall asleep again.

She was still groggy from midnight mommy duty and just about to take her first sip of coffee when she heard what Lee had said. "What did you tell her?" she asked.

"I told her the truth—that you were giving Avery a bath at the time and I would tell you she called."

"Thanks," she uttered. *Damn, she's persistent!*

"Are you going to call her back this time?"

"I don't know." Rachel sipped her coffee delicately, barely able to swallow.

"You know, Nick's not going to be easy today. Maybe we could all just hang out at home together. I don't have to work today."

Rachel glared at her husband. "You don't need to babysit *both* of us, you know," she whispered. "I'm fine. You should take Avery out."

"Come on, you know that's not my intention," he said softly. "I just know you had a rough night and I don't want you to be more stressed than you already are."

Rachel looked over her shoulder to make sure Avery was still out of earshot. "Why don't you just say what you're *really* thinking?" she said softly but sternly. "You're thinking I'm going to lose it again—this time with one or *both* of my kids in the house."

"I don't think that."

"I'm a good mom," Rachel said abruptly. She put down the coffee and crossed her arms.

"I know you're a good mom," said Lee. "But I also know it's been tough on you lately. You've been stressed out. Do you really want to spend the whole day by yourself with a three-year-old and a baby who's *teething*?"

Rachel sighed. "You may have a point."

"Look," he said, placing his hand on top of hers. "It kills me that I can't take your pain away. Sometimes you go to some really dark places, and I don't know how to bring you back. It *kills* me. And I can't *do* anything about it. But I can at least try to take some of the burden off your shoulders."

I hate it when he's right. "I'm sorry." She placed her other hand over his. "I'm just *really* tired."

"I know." He squeezed her hand and kissed it. "How about this? Why don't you just relax in here for a little bit. Enjoy your coffee. I'll play with Avery for a little while and I'll get Nick when he wakes up."

"Sounds good," she yawned.

Lee stood up and kissed Rachel's forehead. Then he took the baby monitor that had been sitting on the kitchen table and carried it into the living room.

For a few minutes, she sat alone and sipped her coffee. She breathed slowly, listening to the background noise from the TV and her daughter's giggling, which brought a much-needed smile to her face.

Suddenly, the phone rang.

"I'll get it!" Rachel stood up with her coffee still in hand. She looked at the caller ID window of the landline phone. The words "Deborah Dixon" stared back at her. It rang a few more times.

She's just going to keep on calling. You might as well get it over with.

On the fifth ring, Rachel picked up the receiver. "Hello."

"Rachel! H-Hi, it's Mom."

"I know," she said, devoid of emotion. "How are you?"

"Well," Rachel's mom stammered, "I-I'm okay. Um, how are you?"

"Fine," she said, sipping her coffee. *At least, it was fine until you called.*

"So the reason I called was because…I know Halloween is right around the corner and I was wondering, um, if there's any way you'd consider bringing the kids *here* to go trick-or-treating."

Rachel closed her eyes and shook her head.

"Are you there?" asked her mom.

"Why would I drive the kids all the way over there when they can just trick-or-treat around *our* neighborhood?"

"Well, I'd hardly consider myself welcomed to go *there* and tag along with you guys."

She remained silent.

"I see," Deborah said, clearly disappointed. "Well, in that case, could you possibly send me pictures of the kids in their costumes?"

"I'll post them on Facebook."

"Okay… You know, Rachel, when you accepted my friend request, I thought perhaps that meant everything was okay between us."

"I don't need our relatives asking a bunch of questions, so I accepted it."

"*I* still have questions, Rachel. I still don't know what I did to cause this animosity."

Stay calm. Don't get angry. She inhaled deeply. "Listen, I can't get into all that right now. I've got to go."

"Okay, well, call me sometime, Rachel… I love you."

Rachel hung up. *If you loved me, you wouldn't have left me there.*

Chapter 12

Once again, Kate found herself waiting. She was in the OB-GYN exam room, naked from the waist down except for a pair of socks to keep her feet warm and a paper gown draped over her lap. The draft in the room coupled with her anxiety made her shiver. The walls were covered with informational posters about everything from parts of the female anatomy to the prevention of STDs and unwanted pregnancies. The images conspired to remind her how real the situation was.

There was a gentle knock on the door, and Dr. Wyatt entered the room.

"Hey, Kate." She smiled and put her hand on Kate's shoulder. "Well, this is a surprise!"

You're telling me.

"How are you feeling?"

"Okay, I guess. Just tired all the time."

Dr. Wyatt chuckled and nodded. "I remember those days."

Kate pressed her lips together.

"Well, your blood test, of course, came back positive. You're definitely pregnant. So, congratulations."

Thanks?

"We'll do a sonogram to figure out how far along you are and see how everything looks, okay?"

"Okay."

The doctor instructed Kate to lie back and scoot her bottom down to the edge of the table. Her legs were placed in stirrups. She picked up a wand and covered it with a condom, which Kate found terribly ironic under the circumstances. The condom was then coated with lubricant.

"This will be cold," the doctor warned. "Are you ready?"

Kate nodded. *Not really, but go ahead.*

Dr. Wyatt inserted the wand slowly and moved it around for a few seconds. "Okay, so I'm just trying to get an image here on the monitor." She tapped the screen with her free hand, which prompted Kate to look.

At first, all Kate could see was a snowy black-and-white blob with strange shapes moving around the screen. But once the doctor moved the wand into the correct position, she was able to make out an image. It was round and layered, somewhat resembling a sore throat lozenge.

The doctor pointed to the image and drew a circle around the outermost layer. "So *this* is the amniotic sac right here." She then moved her finger inward toward the center of the shape. "The embryo is right here." The excitement grew in her voice. Then she pointed dead center to something that appeared to be moving. It was like a little ball opening and closing at about a hundred miles an hour. "And do you see that little flicker…right here in the middle? Well *that*, my dear, is your baby's heartbeat."

Kate couldn't move or speak.

"Are you okay?" Dr. Wyatt asked.

She sighed and looked at her doctor. "I have a *baby*?"

The doctor smiled. "Well, not *technically* yet, but you do have one growing inside you."

Kate felt a tear welling up in her right eye. She quickly wiped the tear away before her doctor could see. All she could do was stare at the monitor in silence, trying to make sense of the unfamiliar emotion that overwhelmed her.

"Don't worry," Dr. Wyatt assured her. "We'll take lots of pictures so you can share this with whomever you want."

Adam. Kate's heart ached. *How do I tell him?*

Chapter 13

Daphne looked up at Renee. They were sitting across from each other in the hospital cafeteria. To Daphne's surprise, Renee had walked from her room to the elevator and from the elevator to the lobby without assistance. Though her pace was still slow, it was a vast improvement from requiring a walker or an arm to hold on to. Her appetite was returning to normal as well. She was enjoying a bowl of vegetable soup while Daphne picked around a chicken salad sandwich with sprouts.

"So...what was the name of the church you went to growing up?" she asked.

Renee was caught off guard and nearly spilled the spoonful of soup that she was about to put in her mouth. She stared at Daphne with a perplexed look and slowly laid the spoon down. "Where did *that* come from?"

Lie. Tell her whatever you have to. "Oh, I don't know," Daphne said. "It's just been a while since we've talked about the past. It's something I've been thinking about, and I was curious." *Good. That's not a total lie.*

Renee nodded and smiled at Daphne. "It was called Holy Trinity."

Daphne suddenly remembered and slapped herself on the forehead. "Of course!"

Renee took a spoonful of soup and continued, "I went there from elementary school through high school. But after I graduated, I moved away for college.

"And tell me again about your friend...Angelina?"

52

"Angie?" said Renee. "That's what we used to call her...before she joined the order, I mean."

Daphne chuckled. "Yeah. I guess 'Sister Angie' doesn't have quite the same cache, huh?"

Renee laughed. "Not really."

"But you guys stayed friends after she became a nun, right?"

"As much as we could, I guess. We stayed in touch for a while, but over time we sort of grew apart. I haven't spoken to her in over... thirty years."

Daphne gulped. "That's a long time." *Change the subject.*

"So I have some news," said Renee. She put down her spoon and folded her hands.

Phew! "What is it?"

"I may be going home soon."

Daphne's eyes nearly bugged out of her skull. "What? When?"

"If I pass inspection, I'll be leaving on Thursday."

Daphne's mouth hung open in disbelief. "*This* Thursday? *Thanksgiving?*"

Renee beamed.

"Wow! Why didn't you tell me sooner?"

"I wanted it to be a surprise."

"Well, mission accomplished!"

"Hey, we couldn't help overhearing," a young woman at the next table said. She was sitting across from a young man who was clearly her significant other. "That's awesome!" Congratulations."

"Thanks," Renee said.

Okay. Too loud, Daphne. Get a hold of yourself. She's going home. Great! But keep it in.

Renee continued, "The doc just wants to do one more scan to make sure I'm in the clear."

"This is amazing," Daphne whispered.

"Obviously, I wanted you to be the first to know."

"So do you need me to come pick you up, or—"

"No, no. I'm going to have one of my neighbors pick me up and bring me home. You won't have to do a thing. Just...live your life. Do your thing. I'll keep you posted as I make plans."

Daphne sighed. "Well, we're having dinner together on Thursday one way or another."

"Yes, ma'am."

"Let me give you a hug before I leave." Daphne stood up and moved closer. "Can you make it back upstairs by yourself?"

"No problem," she said, standing up and hugging Daphne tightly and longer than usual. She whispered in her ear, "I'm so thankful."

Daphne could feel the tears forming. *Get a grip, Daphne.* She stepped back and squeezed Renee's shoulders. "Me too. I'll see you soon, okay?" And with that, she grabbed her handbag and started making her way toward the exit.

Before she opened the door to leave, Daphne turned and looked back at Renee, who was standing by the elevator. She kept watching as the doors opened, and Renee stepped inside. She watched her push the button for the fourth floor and wait. The doors finally closed, and she was out of sight.

After that, Daphne bolted. She power walked all the way to her car, keeping her head down the entire time. Once she was outside, she unlocked the car, grabbed the door handle, and threw it open. She jumped in and slammed the door shut. Her lips began to shake. *There's no one around. Let it out.*

She leaned her head on the steering wheel and sobbed. She couldn't stop.

It's okay. She's gonna be okay. She's going home. It's over.

She continued to sob uncontrollably for several minutes. Every emotion that she had suppressed for nearly two years finally came to the surface. All of the months of worrying and waiting for answers and watching Renee get weaker, to the point where she almost lost her, had led up to this moment. Daphne couldn't fight it anymore. As she cried, her face became completely saturated with tears, and her nose was so full that she could no longer breathe through it.

She grabbed her handbag and fished out a pouch of tissues. Then she used one to blow her nose and wipe her face, removing some of her makeup in the process. For once, she didn't look in the mirror to see how she looked. She just sat for a few more minutes until she caught her breath.

And just before she drove away, she closed her eyes tightly and whispered, "Thank you."

Chapter 14

Rachel sat in Dr. Nova's office. It was at the psychologist's home in a small waterfront community. Everything was just as she remembered:

There was a multicolored area rug in the center of the room. The plush armchair where patients sat was in a corner sandwiched between a large oak bookcase and a small end table, which was a resting place for a box of tissues. A matching oak table lined the wall across from the bookcase. There was a window on the same wall that was covered with simple white drapes. In the corner opposite from the patient chair, there was another end table for the doctor's day planner and a coaster for her water tumbler. Beside that was a hard chair for the doctor herself.

Rachel waited quietly while Dr. Nova signed the insurance form confirming their session and then placed it in her inbox to be faxed to her billing company later. As she took her seat across from Rachel, she removed her reading glasses and laid them on the end table.

"So, Rachel?" she began. "It's been a long time. How have you been?"

"I'm here, aren't I?" she joked.

Dr. Nova chuckled briefly. "True."

"You said if it happened again, I should call."

"And it happened again."

Rachel nodded.

"What happened, Rachel?"

She sighed deeply and shut her eyes. "I was doing fine for the longest time. I even started going to that support group I told you about."

"ACDP?"

"Right," said Rachel, whose eyes were now open again.

There was a silence for a moment.

"Rachel, was something said at one of the meetings that triggered it?"

"I think it was what *I* said."

Dr. Nova furrowed her brow.

"I shared my story."

The doctor's eyebrows were raised now. "How much did you share?"

"The part about *how* my father died. I didn't talk about what happened after that." Rachel looked down at her knees. "I figured that part was irrelevant."

"Well," said Dr. Nova, "in terms of the support group, you're probably right, but it may be hard for you to think about your dad without thinking of the other."

Rachel shifted in her seat. Her hands remained firmly clasped together. Her breathing became heavy.

"It's okay," the doctor assured. "Just tell me, was it the same thing? The shower?"

Rachel nodded abruptly.

"Okay. So it seems pretty obvious that when you shared your story, it opened a Pandora's box to the memories of that period in your life."

Rachel couldn't stop her tears from falling. She grabbed a tissue. "How could I be so *stupid*?"

"It's not stupid! You obviously *needed* to talk about it, so you did."

"Yeah! And now I brought all those other memories to the surface." She wiped her tears and blew her nose. "Damnit! Does it *ever* go away?"

"Do you remember what I told you about that?"

"That the psyche doesn't recognize the passage of time."

"Exactly. With something as powerful as what you went through, there's a part of you that will always be seven years old."

"Well, that sucks."

"I know."

Rachel sighed deeply. "So what do I do?"

For a moment, Dr. Nova said nothing.

Here it comes, thought Rachel.

"You need to get closure. I know we've talked about it before, but I can't stress it enough."

"And I know you're right, but *how* do I do that?"

"You *know* how."

"So do I look my mom in the eye and tell her she's responsible for the worst thing that ever happened to me?"

"Well, I think if you're honest with yourself, you'll know only *one* person was responsible for that. And, Rachel, it *wasn't* your mom. It's just easier to put it on her because she's there."

"Well, I certainly can't confront the *other* person."

"Why not? You're a grown woman. You can handle it."

"Just like that? I mean, that's crazy!"

"Have you ever heard the phrase 'crazy enough to work'?"

"How would I even *find* him?"

"Have you ever t*ried*? For all you know, he could still be living in the same house."

The house. Please don't mention that house!

"You can't avoid it forever," the doctor went on. "If not confronting him face-to-face, at least—"

Rachel began to scratch her hands and wrists, which were already red with hives. Her breathing quickened, and she shook like a leaf.

"Okay," Dr. Nova said, clenching her heart, "I'm sorry. Subject closed."

Rachel closed her eyes and took a deep breath. She stopped scratching herself.

"I'm sorry if I pushed too hard."

58

"It's okay. I know I have to deal with it *someday*. Just...not today."

* * *

At home, Avery was coloring at the table while Lee cooked. Nick was down for his late afternoon nap, giving Lee just enough time to prepare dinner before he woke up. Lee was pulling the last of the hamburgers off the indoor grill with a spatula. He slid them onto a plate and into the microwave to stay warm. Next, he opened the oven door to check on the onion rings.

"Daddy?" said Avery.

"Yes, sweetie?"

"Can we have spaghetti for dinner?"

Lee froze. Suddenly, he realized that the heat of the oven was burning his face. He closed it and cleared his throat. "What made you think of that?"

"Well, we had spaghetti for lunch at school today, and I really like it. Can we have it for dinner, Daddy?"

"What's the matter?" he joked. "Don't you like Daddy's hamburgers?"

Avery giggled. "I love your burgers, Daddy! But can we have spaghetti tomorrow?"

Lee walked over to the table and sat down in front of his young daughter. "Well, you see, Avery, Mommy doesn't like spaghetti."

"But, Daddy, sometimes I have to try things *I* don't like."

He laughed. "That's true, honey, but this is different." He sighed and his tone became more serious. "You see, spaghetti is a...trigger... for Mommy."

"Like the *Winnie the Pooh* Tigger, Daddy?"

"No," Lee shook his head. "No. A *trigger*." He bowed his head, regretting having to explain the matter to a three-year-old. "A trigger is something that reminds someone of a time they were really hurt. So if Mommy is around spaghetti, it makes her very sad."

Avery's eyes widened. "I don't want Mommy to be sad, Daddy."

"Me neither." Lee smiled warmly and rubbed her head.

She became thoughtful for a moment. "Can I still have it for lunch at school?"

He laughed. "Sure! Have all the spaghetti you want at school. Enjoy!"

"Yay!" She beamed and went back to coloring.

With a heavy heart, Lee stood up and walked back to the kitchen. He grabbed a potholder, opened the oven door, and pulled out the tray of onion rings, setting them on a cooling rack. As soon as he was done, Nick's cooing voice could be heard through the monitor. Avery jumped out of her chair and ran to Lee's side so she could go with him to get her baby brother.

Chapter 15

Kate walked through the doors of a different restaurant. The seating hostess greeted her and led her to a booth for two, where Kate sat and waited alone, staring out the window.

She watched and listened as families with children walked up and down the sidewalk outside. They giggled and licked ice cream cones. Sometimes they took turns chasing one another. They looked so happy.

What's that like? she wondered.

A short while later, Kate looked up and saw Adam walking in. She watched him for a moment, admiring how attractive he was—dark hair, rugged yet boyish face. He reminded her a bit of Russell Crowe. Apparently, he'd come straight from work, judging from the dress pants, long sleeve shirt and tie he was wearing. His brown eyes scanned the room for a moment until they caught sight of Kate. She smiled bravely and waved for him to come over. The hostess came up at that moment and greeted him. He told her he was meeting someone and motioned toward Kate. Seeing that her assistance was not required, the young girl retreated.

As Adam approached the table, his head was slightly hunched forward, and his hands were tucked deep in his pant pockets.

"Hi," he said with an awkward smile as he sat down across from her. He took his hands out of his pockets and folded them on top of the table.

"Hey," said Kate.

"I wasn't sure you were going to call me back," he said.

"Neither was I."

The waitress interrupted, "Hi, my name's Tammy, and I'll be serving you tonight. Can I start you guys off with some drinks?"

"Ah, just water for me," Kate answered, "with no ice."

"And for you, sir?" The waitress turned to Adam with dreamy eyes. A twinge of discomfort filled the air. Adam looked at Kate and then at the waitress.

"Pepsi, please," he replied. As soon as the words left his mouth, his eyes went right back to Kate. The waitress looked disappointed at the realization that Adam seemed unavailable. "Coming right up," she said, walking away.

"She's subtle," Kate joked. They both laughed for a moment.

"I'm really glad you called me," he started.

"Well," she said with her head down. "I don't want you to get the wrong idea—"

"I know," said Adam. "I know how it is. You're super independent. You don't want to have any major emotional attachments. I get all that."

Kate looked up. "But?"

"But can I ask you a question?"

She nodded.

"Is it working? Is going through life not connecting with anyone working for you?"

Kate was speechless for a moment. *Say something. Answer him.* Suddenly, she found herself dropping the bomb. "I'm pregnant."

Just then, the waitress appeared with the drinks. Thankfully, it seemed like she missed Kate's announcement.

"Okay, I have your water and your Pepsi," the waitress said and placed the drinks on the table. "Do you guys need a minute?"

Without hesitation, Adam answered, "We're going to need several minutes." The look on his face was hard to decipher. His voice was as serious as a heart attack. The waitress said nothing more before walking away.

Kate stared at Adam. *Is he mad? Is he happy? What's he thinking?*

"You're pregnant?" he repeated in a whisper.

Kate nodded again and swallowed.

"And it's…?" Adam pointed to himself.

"Yes," she whispered.

"That *one night*?"

Her head dropped. It was too much. She wanted to run out of the restaurant. Never look at him again. Just run away and sort out the whole baby situation by herself. But her body felt like it was glued to her seat.

"I thought you were…you know, *using* something," said Adam.

"What do you mean?"

"You know," he raised his voice a touch, "the pill. An IUD. *Something* for protection."

"Why would you automatically *assume* that?"

"Because you never stopped once. You never asked me if *I* had anything, so I figured we were safe."

"Well, I'm sorry." Her voice became defensive. "It was my first time, and I didn't know the protocol."

"Damnit, Kate! Didn't they teach you that in high school? You know, whatever high school you went to after you disappeared?"

Kate looked away, feeling like she'd been stabbed in the heart.

"What are you gonna do?"

"Well—" she started to say. Suddenly, she remembered the sonogram pictures she had in her purse from her doctor's appointment. She reached for them and laid them on the table.

Adam's eyes bulged.

"I don't *know* what to do…but, look!" She pointed to the dot in the center of the round mass. "That's the heart!"

Adam picked up the roll of pictures and carefully examined the one Kate had been pointing to. He said nothing.

"Its *heart* is beating. It's *alive*. I don't know what to do. I'm not *mother material*. I don't even *remember* my moth—" She stopped and put her hand over her face. She could feel herself about to break down crying. *Breathe, Kate…just breathe.*

"Okay," Adam said calmly, "let's just…take a minute."

Kate wiped away a tear. "Adam, what do I do?" She beckoned with her sparkling green eyes.

"Wish I knew." He shrugged. "I feel lost."

That makes two of us.

Chapter 16

It was Thanksgiving Day. Deborah sat on the living room couch in her pajamas. She flipped through the pages of a photo album and held a glass of red wine in her hand. The pictures of her with her late husband reminded her of how handsome he was and how in love they had been. She smiled and laughed to herself, while she wiped her tears away and sipped her wine.

As she continued turning the pages, she came across pictures of Rachel when she was first born. Her husband had beamed with pride when he first held her in the hospital. Then later, he showed that same pride when she crawled for the first time and then walked. He was by her side when she rode a two-wheeler for the first time and on her first day of kindergarten.

Deborah kept turning the pages. Pretty soon, she came to a point in the album where there were no more pictures of her husband. There were only pictures of Rachel. She looked at her daughter's face in the photographs. The light in her eyes that had been so clear and bright when her father was alive had faded. Deborah's intermittent laughter through her tears stopped. All she felt now was sadness.

Deborah came to a picture of Rachel outside their house the morning of her first day of second grade. She wore a short-sleeved white polo shirt, khaki capris, and new sneakers. Her pink *Alvin and the Chipmunks* backpack was over one shoulder, and she was clearly forcing a smile.

As Deborah looked closer, she saw a charm dangling on a gold chain around Rachel's neck: ST ENDS.

It jogged Deborah's memory to the day she saw Rachel wearing it for the first time.

* * *

It was about a month after Deborah had started working at the factory. She picked up Rachel from the Marshalls' house and asked how her day was.

"Fine," Rachel responded from the back seat. She fastened her safety belt and stared out the window.

"That's good," said Deborah.

Rachel didn't say anything else the entire way home, and Deborah was too exhausted after being on her feet all day to engage in further conversation. She turned on the radio, and they listened to music.

When they arrived at home, Deborah tried again to break Rachel's silence.

"Would you like to help me cook dinner?"

Rachel sighed. "Actually, is it okay if I just watch TV?"

"But you always enjoy cooking with me," said Deborah. "Maybe it'll cheer you up."

Rachel shook her head and disappeared into the living room.

Deborah went into the kitchen and started cooking.

About an hour later, the kitchen was filled with the aroma of tomatoes and garlic.

Deborah's stomach rumbled. She stuck her head into the living room and announced happily, "Dinner's ready!" Surely the sight of her favorite meal on the table would raise Rachel's spirits.

Rachel sluggishly pointed the remote at the TV and turned it off. Then she slowly made her way to the kitchen and sat down.

"Do you want milk or water with dinner, sweetheart?"

"Water's fine," she answered glumly.

Deborah would ordinarily emphasize the importance of using the word *please*, but in this case, it seemed uncalled for. She poured Rachel a glass of water and placed it in front of her.

"Thank you," she said.

"You're welcome," Deborah smiled. She grabbed a clean plate for herself and began to assemble her meal. She noticed that Rachel was just sitting there, not touching her food. It was as if she were in a trance, and Deborah didn't know how to bring her out of it. She noticed a necklace around Rachel's neck that she had never seen before.

"Oh, that's a pretty charm, Rachel. Did Baylee give that to you?"

Rachel gulped and nodded.

"Well, I guess you guys are getting along then, huh? That's one of those 'BEST FRIENDS' charms, right?"

"Uh-huh."

"Rachel," Deborah said desperately, putting down her fork. "What's the matter? You haven't even touched your spaghetti."

Rachel paused and looked at her plate, as if it was making her feel nauseated. "Mom," she said softly without making eye contact.

"What is it, sweetie?"

Her face appeared as though she wanted to say something, something important, but instead she said, "I'm...not hungry. Can I please go take a shower?"

Deborah was puzzled. "Are you sure?" She looked at the clock on the microwave. "It's only five thirty."

Rachel nodded. "I know. I just want to get clean. Is that okay?"

Once again, Deborah couldn't find the strength to argue with her child. "Well, okay. Go ahead. Then maybe after that you can try to eat something. I don't want you to go hungry."

"'Kay," Rachel said as she left the table in haste.

Deborah sat at the table by herself and took a bite of spaghetti and meatballs. She chewed it slowly and swallowed. Not being able to stop worrying about her daughter, she put the fork down and got up. She walked out of the kitchen. As she turned the corner and entered the hallway, she could hear the shower running. Then she noticed something strange. It appeared as though Rachel had removed her clothes in the hallway on her way to the bathroom and left them scattered all over the carpet.

"Why would she do that?" she heard herself say out loud. She charged down the hall up to the bathroom door and balled her hand into a fist. Just before she started pounding on the door, she stopped herself.

Tell her to pick up these clothes and put them in the hamper where they belong!

No, no, she's obviously had a rough day. Just let her be. Don't start a fight.

If Glenn was here, he would get Rachel to pick up her clothes.

But Glenn's not here! He'd dead! Rachel is all I've got! And I can't lose her too!"

Deborah couldn't fight back her tears. She went to her bedroom and locked the door. For ten minutes, she was huddled on the floor, sobbing.

God, help me, please! I don't know what to do! Something is wrong with my baby, but what? Please help me!

* * *

Deborah blinked and realized that she still had the glass of wine in her hand. She sighed and placed it on the end table, relieved that she hadn't spilled any on the couch.

She looked at the picture of Rachel on the day that she was to start second grade.

"What the hell happened, Rachel?" she whispered as if the picture could hear her.

"What *happened* to you?"

Chapter 17

Daphne rolled over onto her right side and tucked the bed-sheet under her arm. She exhaled slowly and shut her eyes, letting the afterglow wash over her. Conrad, who was lying behind her, wrapped his arm around her waist. Daphne could feel his body pressed against her back. The smell of his skin was intoxicating.

Ugh! You idiot! You said you weren't gonna do this anymore.

But it's so damn easy! I text him. He comes over. We end up in bed. It's that simple.

With you, nothing is simple.

Conrad's voice, with his alluring English accent, broke through, "Are you glad you texted me?"

Absolutely! She cleared her throat. "Maybe."

They both laughed.

"You know, I quite fancy you."

She flipped over to face him. "You don't fancy *me*. You fancy *it*."

"It?" he asked, furrowing his brow and propping himself up on his elbow.

"Yes, *it*," said Daphne. "This *thing* we keep doing."

"Can't I fancy both?" He leaned in and stroked her forehead with his index finger.

For a moment, she quietly stared off into space and rubbed his chest.

"What's on your mind, love?"

Relax. Don't read into it. "Renee," she answered.

"Well, I thought you said she's improved."

"She has. In fact, she came home a few weeks ago.

"That's fantastic!" He kissed her hand.

Daphne smiled crookedly.

"You don't seem relieved."

"Oh, I am. It's just that…I sort of *did* something while she was in the hospital. And now I'm starting to wonder if it was the right decision."

"Sell off her belongings at auction, did you?"

"No!" She laughed.

"Come on then, talk to me."

Daphne sighed deeply. She sat up and leaned back against the headboard. "I…hired an investigator…to find my birth mother."

"And?"

"And now that Renee's home, I wonder if there's room in my life for *both* of them."

"Hmm," Conrad huffed pragmatically. "So what you're saying is, you no longer feel like you're going to lose Renee, so there's no reason now to look for your real mum. Is that right?"

"I wouldn't exactly put it that way."

"All right then, let me ask you this—why *did* you start looking for your real mum?"

"I don't know."

"Well, there's a first." He kissed her shoulder. "Aren't you always 'inside your head' and analyzing things?"

She squinted. "Don't *you* ever analyze things? Don't you ever look for meaning in what's happening?"

"No." He smiled. "I'm English. We don't think that way. Also, I'm a man, who again doesn't think that way."

Daphne felt her blood getting warm. She crossed her arms. "It's a good thing you're cute."

He only stared at her, unwavering.

"I guess when things started to get really bad, I got scared. I realized if something happened to Renee, I would be alone."

The corners of Conrad's mouth dropped.

"First, my birth mother leaves me. Then my adopted dad leaves me. If Renee left me, too, I'd be without *any* parents."

He pressed his lips together and nodded sympathetically.

"I'm not saying that my birth mom could have *replaced* Renee, but maybe it would have made it hurt a little less."

"So now that she's out of hospital, suddenly the need to find your real mum goes away?"

"Actually, no, it doesn't," said Daphne. "But I just don't know how I feel about it now."

"You think too much." He kissed her and settled in under the covers. "If you ask me, you should finish what you've started. You can't go back now. So just do it and see what happens." He laid his head down and closed his eyes. His face appeared completely content.

Daphne gazed upon the handsome face of her no-strings-attached man friend.

Conrad...Conrad... Why can't I be more like you?

Chapter 18

Rachel arrived home at five thirty in the evening. It was Tuesday. Per usual, Lee had kept the kids for the day so that she could have some time to herself. As she entered the house, Rachel could hear Avery giggling in the living room.

In the foyer, Rachel took off her sneakers and placed them alongside the other shoes that were lined up against the wall. She crept around the corner and peeked at her daughter from the wall that separated the living room and the kitchen. There she was in her play yard, brushing her doll's hair like an angel.

Before Avery could see her, Rachel snuck into the kitchen. Lee was loading the dishwasher when he looked up and saw her. He stopped, winked at her, and then continued his task. Nick, who was sitting in his high chair, had just finished his dinner of pureed vegetables and pasta. He kicked his legs excitedly at the sight of his mother and beamed, revealing a handful of tiny teeth.

"Hi, baby," Rachel said sweetly. She leaned in and kissed her son's forehead and stroked his short but curly blond hair.

A glob of spit-up suddenly oozed from his mouth and landed on the tray of his high chair.

"Uh-oh!" She laughed. "Someone's got a little spit-up."

"I'll clean him up, babe," Lee assured her.

"It's okay," Rachel said. "It's the least I can do."

Lee grabbed a box of baby wipes from the counter and walked over to them. "Woman," he said jokingly. "I've *got* this."

Rachel stood up slowly and sighed.

Before she could protest, Lee kissed her forehead and said, "Go. I've got this. Go do your thing."

"Well, okay. I could use a hot bath. I'm just gonna go say hi to Avery first."

"Take your time," he said, beginning to wipe off Nick's face.

Avery was brushing her doll's hair and humming sweetly.

Rachel walked into the living room quietly and stepped into the play yard, behind Avery. "Hi, baby girl." She kneeled.

Avery turned. "Mommy," she exclaimed, dropping her doll. She immediately threw her arms around Rachel's neck and hugged her tight, which nearly knocked her over.

"Oh my goodness!" Rachel wrapped her arms around her and squeezed. "Did you have a good day today?"

"Look, Mommy!" Avery said as she let go and retrieved her doll. She then placed it on Rachel's lap. Around the doll's neck was a yellow gold chain. There was an old pendant dangling from it with the letters "ST ENDS."

Rachel's heart sank. *Oh God. No!* "W-Where did you get this, Avery?" She held the doll up to her daughter.

"From your jewelry box, Mommy," Avery said softly. She swallowed. "I asked Daddy if I could play with it, and he said yes."

Rachel's cheeks reddened. *What the hell was he thinking? He should have asked me first!* "Avery," Rachel said sternly, removing the necklace from the doll, "you are *not* allowed to play with this necklace. *Ever.* Do you understand me? Not *ever.*"

Avery's little head dropped in shame, unable to bear the look in her mother's eyes. "Yes, Mommy." She sighed.

"Not ever."

"I'm sorry, Mommy." Her voice cracked. Slowly, she looked up at Rachel again. Her brown eyes were wet with tears, and she pouted like a sad puppy.

Rachel's chest ached, as if her heart was literally breaking. *Oh no, my poor baby. I've hurt her feelings.* Rachel hugged her daughter tightly. Avery rested her head on Rachel's shoulder and cried softly. "It's okay, baby. It's okay. I'm sorry too." She sighed. "How about if Mommy finds another necklace for you to put on Betty Lou?"

"Okay," Avery whispered. Her head still rested on Rachel's shoulder.

God, I suck! She pulled away from Avery slowly. Then she wrapped the end of her sleeve around her index finger and used it to dab her daughter's eyes. "Dry those tears, okay?"

Avery breathed deeply and wiped the rest of the tears away with her own sleeves. She sniffed loudly.

"Let me get you a tissue," Rachel offered. She placed one foot outside the play yard and reached for a box of tissues on a nearby end table. Suddenly, she realized that Lee was standing just a few yards away, holding Nick. The couple made eye contact. Rachel saw the look on Lee's face and felt even more remorseful. *He heard.*

Later that evening, after the kids were asleep, Rachel came down the stairs into the living room. Lee was in his recliner, watching TV. As soon as she entered the room, he wasted no time pausing the DVR.

"What the hell was that earlier?" he asked.

Damn it! Rachel raised her hands to shoulder level with her palms forward. "Hey, I didn't yell and I didn't lose control."

"It doesn't matter. She's only *three*."

"Well, if you hadn't let her go into my jewelry box and said yes to her playing with that necklace, *that* wouldn't have happened!"

"Sorry! I assumed if that necklace was important to you, you would've mentioned it by now! What's the big deal?"

Get out of the room, Rachel. Just walk away. Don't make it worse. She turned around and disappeared into the kitchen. She placed her hands on the counter and closed her eyes. For a few minutes, she just breathed slowly in and out. Her body began to feel lighter, almost like she was half-asleep.

* * *

Rachel's mom had just dropped her off at the Marshalls' house for the first time. She was walking around the backyard, which stretched out into the nearby woods. There was a wooden deck at the back of the house, where Baylee liked to hide. Rachel could see her crouched in the darkness beneath the deck, hugging her knees.

"Baylee?" Rachel whispered, getting down on all fours. "What are you doing?"

"Shhh," Baylee whispered back.

Rachel crawled under the deck and sat down beside her new friend. "What are you hiding from?"

Baylee trembled. "My dad."

"Why would you be hiding from your daddy?"

There was no answer.

* * *

"Rachel," Lee said in a gentle voice.

She opened her eyes. Turning around to face him, she wrapped her arms around herself.

"Are you okay?" he asked.

Rachel's glance shifted, as if she was looking at the floor. "That necklace belonged to Baylee."

Lee froze. His eyes widened. "Baylee? You mean—"

"Yes," she interrupted. "*That* Baylee."

There was silence for a moment. The tension was palpable.

Lee was the first to speak again. "Why didn't you ever tell me about it? I mean, you told me about everything else."

"I don't know." She shook her head.

"I don't want to sound insensitive," he said as he stepped forward softly and stood beside her. He rested his foot on one of the cabinets to support his weight. "But why have you kept it all this time? Shouldn't you just get rid of it?"

"I've thought about it," she confessed. "And I've wanted to. Hell, it was *years* before I was even able to take it off."

He nodded.

"I guess I just feel like if I let go of that necklace, I let go of *her* too and I let go of the promise I made to her. I promised I would protect her. I promised I wouldn't tell anyone."

"But you did."

74

Tears welled up in her eyes. "Exactly. It's bad enough that I couldn't protect her. I couldn't even keep my word."

"Rachel, you were *seven*." He put his arm around her shoulder. "You couldn't protect *yourself*, let alone protect *her*. And it was *years* before you told anyone."

"Even so."

Lee hung his head in frustration.

"I don't expect you to understand."

"You're right, I don't understand." He pulled away and stood in front of her. "But here's what I know. It happened a long time ago. You've made it this far, and you're the strongest person I know. But you'll never get over it if you don't let go of it...*all* of it."

Rachel wiped her tears and looked sadly at her husband, much like her daughter had looked at her earlier that evening.

"Get rid of the necklace," he said. "Tell your mom. Let it go."

She sighed. Another tear rolled down her cheek. "I don't know if I can."

Chapter 19

It was almost the end of Kate's shift at the diner. She made sure every inch of the front counter was spotless. After that, she arranged the ketchup bottles and salt-and-pepper shakers. She wiped down the menus and placed each one in just the right spot so that a customer would have it in front of them when they sat down. As she worked, she thought about the lady that had sat at that counter a few months prior, the one who had left her the very generous tip. Kate had hoped to see her again and thank her for her generosity. Night after night, however, there was no such luck.

Once Kate was done with the counter, she moved on to the booths and began the same ritual. She looked up and caught a glimpse of herself in the mirrored double doors that led to the kitchen. The tiny bump in her lower abdomen was not noticeable to the casual observer, but Kate knew all too well that it was there. *You've got to tell Pete and Elizabeth. They're going to find out sooner or later. And it may not be much longer before they can see it.*

She stopped working and sat at the empty booth that she had just cleaned. Her eyes gazed upon the front counter, where Adam sat the day she saw him again after nearly a decade.

* * *

One day, out of the blue, he had walked in and sat at the counter. Kate hadn't noticed who it was at first, only that it was a man. She immediately grabbed her pad and pen and walked over to him. With her eyes down, as usual, she asked, "Hi, can I get you anything to drink, sir?"

"Actually, first you can tell me what happened to Kate Jones," a husky voice answered.

The voice sounded familiar. Kate looked up and recognized him instantly. "Adam?"

They both laughed.

"Oh my gosh!" Kate shook her head and smiled. "I can't believe it's you."

"How long have you worked here?" he asked.

"I guess about...two years now."

"This is crazy because I moved back to town a year ago. My place is just across the street, but it's the first time I've come in."

Kate shrugged. "Small world, I guess."

"So...how have you been? What's new?"

She sighed. "Not much. Just working and living in a lot of different places, but I ended up back here."

"I guess some things never change," he said.

Kate nodded.

"So I know what you're probably going to say, but do you want to get together some time? It doesn't have to be a date. We could just grab a drink or a cup of coffee when you get off work sometime."

She looked into his deep brown eyes for a moment, in a way that she never had before. The truth was, she was tired of saying no.

"Why not?" She shrugged again and smiled.

Adam's eyes widened. "Wow. I guess some things do change."

* * *

Kate suddenly realized that she'd been staring at the counter and people were beginning to stare back. She shook her head and looked up at the clock above the kitchen doorway. It was time for her to leave. She stood up, tossed her apron into the "soiled linen" hamper, and gave the kitchen staff a quick wave.

Someone said, "Good night," but in her daze, she wasn't sure which of the cooks had spoken.

Outside, Kate started her walk home. Dark clouds loomed overhead. It made her think of Adam yet again. To make matters worse, she was standing just a few hundred yards away from the club where they'd met. It was a small dimly light establishment that served beer, wine, and appetizers. It was called Dave's Dive Bar. The place also featured live music most nights of the week and was the perfect place for light conversation. Kate's mind began to drift again.

On that fateful night, Kate had showed up early. To her surprise, Adam was already sitting at the bar, enjoying a beer and bantering with Dave, who was tending the bar that night. She stood at the doorway in a sundress and strappy sandals. Her small satchel purse laid cross-body against her right hip, and she clutched a mini umbrella in her left hand.

Adam did a double take when he saw her. He'd never seen her in a dress before.

Shyly, she waved at him.

He signaled for her to join him.

Her heart began beating faster as she ambled up to the bar.

The bartender was around their age, maybe a few years older. His head was completely shaved, and he sported a neatly shaven goatie. His left eyebrow was pierced. The tattoos up and down both of his arms were made more conspicuous by the black muscle shirt he was wearing.

"Dave," said Adam, "this is my friend Kate, the one I was telling you about. Kate, this is Dave."

Kate extended her hand. "Hi. It's nice to meet you."

"Pleasure." He smiled and shook her hand gently. Despite his outward appearance, his demeanor was sophisticated and friendly. "Can I get you a beer? Or maybe a glass of wine?"

Suddenly, Kate feared that her lack of experience in this department would show. "Umm, I think I'll have a glass of white wine, please."

Luckily, Dave had a list that he whipped out and presented to her. Luckier still, he wasn't afraid to use subtle flirtation to keep the conversation moving. "Well, young lady, you look like you enjoy a *touch* of sweetness but not *too* much. So I'd recommend the Riesling. It's made in house and tends to be just a little drier than most Rieslings. At the same time, it's very smooth."

Kate, unknowingly caught up in the moment, answered back, "Kind of like you?"

Adam burst into laughter, nearly making him spit out some of his beer. Dave's smile, which stretched from ear to ear, didn't falter. "She's tough." He looked at Adam and then back at Kate.

"Riesling would be fine," she said.

Dave snatched the wine list and made it disappear under the bar again like a magician. "Coming right up."

When Dave presented the wine, Kate thanked him and took a small sip. She waited a moment, letting it settle on her tongue. It tasted sweet at first, but then the strength of the alcohol made her mouth tingle and her eyes widen. Suddenly, she looked at Adam and realized he'd been looking at her the whole time.

"Sorry, I just can't believe I'm sitting here with you right now."

Taking another sip, she asked, "So what have you been doing for the past few years?"

"Well, I started out in Gainesville for college. It was a pretty typical experience at first. My dad wanted me to pledge to his fraternity, of course." He rolled his eyes.

"Did you?" asked Kate.

"I checked it out, but it just wasn't for me. That pissed him off. Then later he saw that I was taking electives like World Religions and Psychology. He said 'What the hell does that shit have to do with Business Administration?' I said 'Don't you want me to be a well-rounded individual?' He told me 'No. As long as I'm paying your tuition, you need to focus on your degree. If you want to do that foo-foo crap, do it with your own money.'"

Kate's eyes and jaw dropped. "That seemed a little harsh."

"It was," Adam agreed, "but it was good for me. I decided to leave U of F and go to a community college where my scholarship and credits were transferable. I also got a job to pay the remaining tuition and buy the books I needed. It took a little longer to finish that way, but at least I got out from under my father's thumb."

Kate held her glass up to Adam. "Well, here's to you."

They clinked glasses and drank.

"So what type of degree did you end up getting?"

"I have an associate's degree in Business Administration."

Now Kate couldn't contain her laughter. "You mean after all of *that*, you wound up doing the same thing?"

He raised his hands like he was under arrest. "Hey, I always wanted to get my AA. I just didn't want my father running my life."

"Was he pissed?" Kate asked.

"Extremely."

They both cracked up.

When the laughter died down, Adam changed the subject. "So how about you? What have you been doing for the last nine and a half years?"

"Another Riesling?" Dave interrupted, having seen that her glass was empty.

"Ah, sure," she said haphazardly, preoccupied by Adam's question.

"Another Yingling, bro?" he asked Adam.

"Yes, please."

Suddenly, Kate felt drops of water falling on her head. *Where were they coming from? A leak in the ceiling, perhaps?*

"Kate?" she heard a man's voice saying, but it wasn't Adam. "Kate?"

* * *

She then realized that it was Pete who was calling her name. And the water drops that were hitting her were not from a leaky ceiling. They were drops of rain.

"Kate! Darling, what are you doing standing here in the rain? Are you all right?" He covered her with an umbrella.

How long was I daydreaming? "Hi, Pete. Yes, I'm fine. Is everything okay? Do you need something?"

"I was coming to the house to see you. Ah, you dropped something when you left the restaurant." Pete reached into his pocket and pulled something out. His hand remained closed as he placed the object in Kate's hand. When he pulled his hand away, she looked down in horror. It was a bottle of her prenatal vitamins.

Chapter 20

Rachel was driving to the community center. The sky had been overcast all afternoon, and light rain was starting to drizzle on her car. It had been months since she had first met Daphne and Paul at the ACDP meeting, and she was determined to go back and sit with them. Week after week, she'd start driving there. And every week, she chickened out at the last minute. The shower incident had shaken her confidence, making it harder for her to be around people. And then there was the situation with Avery and the necklace.

That damned necklace! As she drove, she remembered the first time she saw it when she was seven.

* * *

She had just arrived at the Marshalls' home. Baylee was huddled under the deck at the back of the house, hiding. Rachel had just joined her. There had been no answer to the question about why she was hiding from her dad.

Rachel, wanting to change the subject at the time, noticed the gold chain around Baylee's neck. Strangely, it held two pendants. If placed together, they would spell out "Best Friends." "Aren't you supposed to wear one of those and then give the other one to someone else?" she asked.

Baylee looked down at her chest, where the charms lay. "I don't have a best friend... I don't have any friends."

"Why not?" Rachel asked sadly.

Baylee shrugged.

"Well, we're going to the same school this year and we'll be in the same grade. So we can be friends."

Baylee smiled awkwardly.

"I came over to play with you. Do you want to play inside? It's kind of hot out here, even under the deck."

She shook her head no.

Suddenly, they heard the sound of a car door closing.

"I'll be right back," Baylee said abruptly. She crawled quickly to the edge of the deck, sprang to her feet, and ran out of sight.

Rachel waited patiently.

Within moments, Baylee came back and got down on all fours. She looked at Rachel and said. "We can go inside now. My mom is back from the store."

"Okay." Rachel smiled. She followed Baylee into the house to play.

* * *

Rachel suddenly realized she was no longer driving. She was parked outside the community center. It was as if she'd fallen asleep and arrived there by autopilot. Her car's engine was still running. She looked at the clock. It was exactly four thirty. The meeting was about to start.

You'll feel better if you go in.

Her heart was racing a mile a minute. She was sweating. Her cheeks felt hot. She looked in the mirror at herself. Her lopsided bun (which was messier than usual), her shiny complexion, and the dark circles under her eyes would surely give away how she felt on the inside.

It's not a beauty contest. Nobody cares. Just go in.

She wanted to turn the car engine off and go inside. She wanted to smile, greet Paul and Daphne, and sit with them during the meeting. She wanted to hear the inspiring stories of the other people that had suffered loss, just like her. She wanted to invite Daphne and

Paul to have dinner at the quaint little diner a few blocks away. She wanted it more than anything.

But she couldn't move. She looked in the rearview mirror and saw the people arriving at the last minute, running to get inside. She saw one of the volunteers closing the door. No one else went inside.

Then all was quiet. She was alone in a parking lot filled with cars. The world was still. Even the playground across the street that was usually alive with the sounds of children playing was barren. The silence was deafening.

She turned the stereo on, put the gearshift in reverse, and started heading for home.

* * *

A few blocks away, Adam had just walked into Dave's Dive Bar.

"Hey, buddy! How's it going?" Dave called out as soon as Adam approached the bar.

"Not bad," Adam responded.

"The usual, man?"

"Yes, please."

"Coming right up."

Adam sat and waited for a moment. He scanned the dimly lit room. People were drinking, eating, and laughing. They were so care free, much like he and Kate had been that fateful night. His chest began to hurt.

"Here you go, buddy." Dave returned with a beer, which he set in front of Adam. He then placed a glass of Riesling on top of the bar beside Adam's beer with no one there to drink it.

"Thanks." He took a sip and glanced at the empty stool next to him.

"So are you going over there tonight or what?" Dave asked.

Adam sighed. "Who knows?"

"Well, at least call her then."

"I did. It was weeks before she called me back the last time."

"So you're just gonna give up? Just like that?"

"She knows where to find me. If I keep calling, she'll think I'm weird."

Dave chuckled. "No offense, dude, but you *are* weird. You come in every week and order a glass of wine for a date that's not even here."

"If she were here, I'd buy it for her."

"What? I thought you said she was pregnant!"

"Shhh!" Adam looked around to see if anyone had heard, but it seemed like no one did. "Not so loud, man."

"Sorry," Dave whispered.

"I meant, if it were still *that* night…if we were still sitting here like we were, I'd be happy to pay for her wine. So what's the difference?"

"The *difference*," Dave said sternly, "is that that night is *over*, man. You've got to move on!"

"I tip you, don't I?" he said, taking a sip.

"Absolutely." He nodded. "And I appreciate it."

Adam took a long swig of his beer before speaking again. "You're right, though. This makes no sense. I sit here week after week and do this, like I'm trying to relive that night. Then I stand across the street from her house for who knows how long…just staring in that direction. I try to get my legs to move so I can go over there. And then every week, I just end up going home."

"So what's stopping you?"

He shrugged.

Another customer was trying to get Dave's attention. Dave excused himself and got back to work.

Later, on the way to Kate's house, Adam kept thinking about Dave's question.

What's stopping me?… All I have to do is go over there, knock on the door, and talk to her… What do I say to her?… Maybe I don't have to say anything. I can just ask how she's doing and let her do the talking… But she may not want to see me.

He suddenly stopped and turned. He looked across the street at her front porch.

If she doesn't want to see me, then I'm no worse off because she's already not seeing me, right?... Yeah, but...right now, I still have that night. I still remember how she looked at Dave's. I can still see her sitting next to me in that bar stool. I still have the image of her laughing and tucking that one piece of hair behind her ear. If I go over there and things go bad, it'll change... At least this way, it's untainted. There's still hope. I don't want to lose that.

Adam took one last long look at Kate's house before turning around and walking home with the cool wintery breeze blowing on his back.

Chapter 21

The jig was up for Kate. As she stood on the sidewalk, sheltered by Pete's umbrella and looking into his eyes, she knew she couldn't lie anymore. He'd been a father figure to her for the last two years. That was something she'd never had before. She had never betrayed his trust and she couldn't do it now. Pete deserved better, so she fully admitted the truth.

"Darling, when did this happen? Who is the father? Do you need anything? Come, we sit down and talk." He tried to lead her back to the diner.

Kate resisted. "No, Pete. I know you have tons of questions, and I want to answer them. But right now, I really just want to be alone. Is that okay?"

He sighed loudly. The corners of his eyes dropped. "Okay." He nodded and winked. "But we *will* talk, no?"

"You're not angry?" Kate asked, both surprised and relieved.

"What do you think? I was born yesterday? These things happen."

She couldn't help cracking a smile. *Good ole Pete.* "Thank you."

"Ah!" He hugged her. "You let me know what we can do, okay?"

"Okay." She awkwardly accepted his hug.

Pete turned and walked back toward the restaurant. Kate stood for a moment, watching him.

She managed to make it to the house without stopping this time—that is, until she stopped at the front door. She looked at it with disdain.

I'm so stupid! If I had just walked through this door that night, none of this would have happened.

Her memory wandered again.

* * *

She and Adam were still sitting at the bar. Dave had just brought each of them a fresh drink. Kate was thinking about how to answer his previous question: where have you been in the last nine and a half years? While she was still composing her answer, the musician who was performing that night began to speak over the microphone.

"Check…check…one…two… Can you guys hear me?"

A few people applauded. Apparently, he was a regular.

"I'll take that as a yes."

Kate seized the opportunity, turned to Adam, and said, "Maybe we can talk about that another time."

"Sure," he said, taking another swig of beer. He turned his attention to the stage.

Kate swiveled around in her barstool to do likewise.

The musician, in his early twenties, had jet-black hair that was already starting to thin. He wore a button-down gray shirt, relaxed fit jeans, and flip-flops. His fingers gently plucked the guitar strings, warming them up. His toe tapped as he tried to find a rhythm. His body swayed back and forth. He played the first few notes and received applause from some of the other patrons. He started to sing.

Kate leaned back in her barstool, sipped her wine, and listened intently. She became lost in the song. The lyrics and melody were sad yet beautiful. She didn't even realize she'd been swaying gently from side to side in her seat while it played.

Adam couldn't keep his eyes off her. He'd never seen her smile for so long. He'd never seen her look happy at all. And although he'd always found Kate to be pretty, tonight she was stunning.

The song ended. Kate and Adam set their drinks down and clapped loudly for the artist.

A while later, when the musician had finished playing his set, Kate suddenly became aware of the tingling sensation in her fingers. Her head felt a little light, and she began to yawn.

Adam checked his watch to see what time it was. It was still early.

"Sorry." She smiled with embarrassment. "I guess the wine is hitting me pretty hard."

"It's okay." He chuckled. "I'll walk you home. He sprang to his feet and helped her down off her barstool.

On the walk home, they bantered about mutual childhood memories. It had started to rain, and Kate shared her umbrella with Adam, though the rain coming in sideways was wetting their feet.

"Oh my gosh!" Adam said. "Remember the time Mrs. Simmons got her skirt caught in the drawer of her desk when she was looking for the board eraser?"

Kate laughed harder than she had in years. "You mean when we all thought she was gonna crack her head open on the desk?"

"No such luck!"

They both laughed for a moment, not thinking about the fact that they'd already arrived at Kate's front porch. Under the overhang, the umbrella became superfluous. She closed it and laid it against the wall to dry.

"Well," Adam sighed, looking into her eyes. He was shaking. "This was fun."

"Yeah," Kate agreed. *Oh my gosh, is he gonna kiss me?* She began to tremble also. *I think I want him to kiss me.* He gently leaned in and kissed her cheek. A shock wave ran up her spine.

"Well, good night," he said softly. Quickly, he turned and jogged across the street to the partially covered sidewalk and then slowed down and started walking to his apartment.

"Good night," Kate said, although there was no way Adam could have heard her. For a moment, she stared at her front door. She kept waiting for a voice inside of her to say, *Go in, you ding-dong. Just go inside, put on something dry, brush your teeth, and get into bed!* But she heard nothing. All she could think about was the softness of his lips on her cheek and the intoxicating smell of his deodorant when he had leaned in closer.

Suddenly, she turned and took off after him. She didn't even grab her umbrella.

"Adam!" she called to him. But between the distance and the rain, he couldn't hear her.

He was still in her sight, not more than a few hundred yards ahead. There were quite a few people meandering on the sidewalk, so it was hard to catch up. Once she got away from them, she picked up her pace. She could still see him despite the rain that continued to fall on her head. By now, her hair was completely soaked, and she was completely oblivious.

Adam stopped in front of an old antique shop, which had a staircase around the back leading up to an apartment. He grabbed his keys out of his wet pocket and marched up the stairs. By the time he was at the top, Kate was standing on the ground just below.

"Adam!" she called again.

Startled, he jumped and turned to face her. "Geez, you *scared* me."

"I'm sorry. I didn't mean to."

"It's all right." He walked down to the bottom of the stairs again. "Are you okay? What are you doing here?"

She stared into his eyes. "I don't know."

He shook his head, unsure of how to respond.

Kate reached up, grabbed his face, and kissed him. He kissed her back. He held her face gently and turned it. His head moved in the opposite direction. He parted her lips slowly with his thumb and touched her tongue with his. It moved around the inside of her mouth, creating a sensation she'd never felt before. Yet it felt perfectly natural.

"Do you want to come in?" he whispered in her ear.

She nodded.

He took her by the hand and led her up the stairs. He unlocked the door and gestured for her to go in first. Ordinarily, Kate would have been worried about where she could wipe her wet feet, but the combination of the wine, the music which still resonated, and Adam's kiss left her without a care in the world—at least for the next hour.

Adam's hands shook as he locked the door and turned again to face Kate. He held her face in his hands. "Is this real?" he asked her.

Words eluded her. She closed her eyes and savored the feel of his hands on her. And before she knew it, they were kissing again. And this time, they didn't stop.

A few hours later, she woke up in his arms. Their clothes had long since been removed and were scattered around his bedroom. Kate could feel his bare skin pressed against hers. Her head had been lying on his chest for an undetermined length of time. She propped herself up just enough to see his face. She'd never seen anyone look so peaceful and happy. And for a moment, she was too.

As she sat up, however, reality began to creep in. *Oh my gosh! I just lost my virginity to Adam! What was I thinking?!*

She slowly began to pull away, trying not to wake him. Quietly, she crawled out of the bed and tiptoed around the room, grabbing her clothes. When she was fully dressed again, she sat in a nearby chair and watched Adam as he slept.

She thought about how nice he'd been to her. How he'd made her feel something that she never thought she'd experience. Not just sex. She knew eventually she would venture into that territory. But *this*… Her experience may have been lacking, but she knew for sure that it wasn't something people felt every day. In answer to his question: yes, this *was* real. It was *too* real.

I'm so sorry, Adam. She left quietly as he slept happily, no doubt dreaming about her.

* * *

Kate stared at her door again now. She thought about how everything had changed *that* night, when she'd made the decision not to go through it. Instead, she'd gone through a different door, and for the first time, she experienced love. And now the evidence of that night was growing inside her. It had a heartbeat—hers and

91

Adam's. It was all too much. That's why she'd been avoiding Adam. But she wondered how long he would avoid *her*...avoid *both of them*.

Finally, she unlocked the door and went inside. Little did she know that just a short time prior to that, Adam had been on the other side of the street looking at that same door.

Chapter 22

It was the week before Christmas. With Florida winter in full swing, the humidity had settled down to manageable levels, and the temperature was cool enough for early evening walks.

Daphne changed into her athletic wear before she left work and began driving to Renee's house. *I can't believe I'm actually going walking with Renee. Seems like just yesterday she couldn't even get out of bed. Now we're gonna start walking together again!*

When she pulled up to the house, she parked her car in the driveway beside Renee's. The sky was preparing for a beautiful sunset. If they left right away, they could enjoy it during their walk around the neighborhood. As Daphne stepped out of her car and shut the door, she heard a child's giggle. She turned and saw a little boy who was no more than three years old. He was riding a tricycle on the sidewalk in front of Renee's house, while his mom jogged closely behind him. The two of them joked back and forth, and Daphne couldn't help but smile. The mother waved as they passed and smiled back at Daphne. She watched as they continued down the sidewalk and out of sight.

Daphne turned around and walked up to the door, which she knew would be unlocked. "Hello?" she called as she entered. The smell in the air was heavenly. Daphne couldn't tell what it was, but she could tell it was something that she clearly should not eat if she wanted to maintain her slender yet muscular frame. "What smells so good?"

"Pot roast," Renee answered from the kitchen happily. "With cheesy Texas toast fresh from the oven."

Ugh! Sounds so good but so unhealthy.

Be polite. She was nice enough to cook. Just be extra good tomorrow.

Renee lifted the lid off the crockpot and stirred the pot roast. "This will stay warm while we take our walk. And I'm doing the oven trick to keep the bread warm."

Daphne remembered this technique from when she was a child. "So you've preheated the oven, and now you're going to put the bread in and turn the oven off. That way it cooks long enough to get warm and toasty and then stays warm until we get to it."

"You remember." Renee winked, placing the cold bread into the oven.

After that, they set out on their walk. Sure enough, the sun was just starting to set. The sky was decorated with beautiful streaks of pink and orange. The temperature was a perfect sixty-eight degrees. And even though the sun was still out, a few of the neighbors had already turned on their Christmas lights for the evening.

"Isn't it beautiful?" Renee inhaled the early-evening air.

"Sure is," Daphne agreed.

They turned left at the sidewalk and began their usual route: around the sidewalk to the end of the block. Then they'd turn left to take the main street of the subdivision. Next, they'd hike all the way down to where the sidewalk ended, turn around, and stroll back to the house.

When they made the first turn, Daphne began asking questions. "So it's been almost a month since they released you. Have you been back for a checkup?"

Renee shook her head. "No need."

"But you were really sick. Don't they need to check on it once in a while?"

Renee huffed. "Well, typically cancer patients will get checked every few months for the first couple of years when they leave the hospital.

"So you're good till…what, February? March?"

Renee suddenly stopped walking. "Daphne, I just got home." She sounded frustrated. "Let me enjoy myself for a little while before I start thinking about having to go back."

She's right. Quit being insensitive. "I'm sorry."

"It's okay." She patted Daphne on the back and started walking again. After that, she didn't say a word for almost a block.

Is she mad at me? "You okay?"

Renee sighed. "I'm fine…just listening."

Daphne furrowed her brow. "To what?"

"Everything," she answered. "The birds chirping, the sound of cars coming and going, kids playing and laughing…stuff like that."

"You can *hear* all of that?"

"Sure," Renee remarked. "When I was alone in the hospital, sometimes I got tired of watching TV and listening to music. At one point, books only made me sleepy, and I was tired of sleeping—as odd as that may sound. So I started listening to see what I could hear if I turned the noise down. And I found out there are a lot of beautiful sounds that can be heard if we just listen. It's not that hard once you try it."

Kind of like what that professor was talking about at the meeting.

"So are you seeing anyone lately?" Renee suddenly asked. They reached the end of the sidewalk and were turning around.

She grinned. "Mmm…kind of."

Renee elbowed her. "Really? You've been holding out on me."

"Well, you know, it's just one of those things. I mean, I like spending time with him, but I'm just not sure where it's going."

"You like to keep your options open, huh?"

"You could say that." Daphne nodded. *It's much safer that way.*

"Are you hungry?" Renee asked Daphne when they walked back into the house.

"Absolutely." She sighed. *Always.*

Renee went into the kitchen and started washing her hands.

Daphne occupied herself by taking out her cell phone and checking her messages.

After her hands were clean and dry, Renee grabbed an oven mitt from the countertop. Carefully, she opened the oven door. She bent forward, grabbed the bread, and stood up again. Suddenly, she dropped the tray onto the stove range and stepped backward. She quickly put her hands on the counter to keep from falling.

Daphne ran to her side and put her arms around her shoulders. "Hey, are you okay? What happened?"

"Phew," Renee said, shaking her head. "Just a dizzy spell. I think I stood up too fast after I bent down." She patted Daphne's hand. "I'm fine now."

"Are you sure?"

"Yes. I'm fine." She started taking out the bowls, plates, and utensils. "Why don't you go wash your hands?"

"Sure," Daphne complied. She entered the guest bathroom and shut the door. She turned on the water. As she waited for it to get warm, she pumped foaming hand soap into her palms and began scrubbing rigorously.

Maybe this isn't the best time to go on my trip.

Don't worry. Everything is fine.

That's what she says, but she could have collapsed just then.

But she didn't. If there was a problem, the doctor wouldn't have sent her home. Everyone gets dizzy from time to time. Don't cancel the trip. She finished rinsing her hands and dried them.

Then she put on a brave smile and joined Renee in the dining room.

Chapter 23

I t was Christmas Day. Deborah picked up her cell phone for the third time that morning, wondering what she should say. What would she say if she had to leave a message? What would she say if her daughter actually picked up the phone for a change?

Don't think. Just dial. It'll come to you.

She opened her contacts folder and scrolled down. She tapped the name Rachel. It rang and rang.

The voicemail message started playing. "Hi, this is Rachel. Sorry I—"

Deborah hung up the phone and dropped it on the coffee table in front of her. She cupped her face in her hands and breathed deeply.

This is ridiculous! It's Christmas! I should be with her. I should be with my grandbabies. How did this go so wrong?

* * *

Deborah looked at Rachel in the rear view mirror. She was sitting in the back seat of their old, used Volvo—the only car she could afford after Glenn died. She'd sold off everything of value, including two new cars, in case a job didn't come through right away. It had been terrifying for those first couple of months. There was no way of knowing when something might open up, or if it would pay enough to support her and Rachel. Meals that used to be just for fun like macaroni and cheese with diced hot dogs had become the norm. Rachel never did complain, or even question the change, but Deborah knew the reason for it, and it broke her heart.

"Why do you have to go, Mommy?" she whined.

"I told you, Rachel." Deborah had said as gently as she could. "Mommy has to keep working."

"To pay our bills?" Rachel had asked.

"That's right."

"Well, what if *I* help pay the bills?"

Deborah chuckled softly. "And how would you do that?"

Rachel pondered for a moment, staring out of the car window. "It *is* hot outside. Maybe I can open a lemonade stand."

"Well, maybe that's something you and Baylee can do together."

There was no sound from the back seat. Rachel clenched her half of the "BEST FRIENDS" charms in her small fist.

"That would be fun, right?"

"Mommy, what if I came with you to work?" she asked hopefully. "I promise I won't bother you. I can even help. Please, Mommy."

"Sorry, sweetheart. There're no kids allowed at work. It's a factory, and you might get hurt."

"Oh," she said sadly.

They drove in silence the rest of the way.

When they arrived at the Marshalls' house a few minutes later, Deborah put the car in park and kept the engine running. She turned around and looked at Rachel. Her arms were crossed in front of her angrily. Her face was pressed against the door.

"Rachel, I need to go, honey." Once again, she tried to be gentle. "I can't be late."

"Mommy, I can't stay here today."

Deborah sighed impatiently. "Why not?"

"I'm sick." She wrapped her arms around her stomach and made a face so as to appear nauseated.

"I'm sure once you get inside and start playing, you'll feel better."

"No, I won't!" she yelled.

Deborah felt her face getting warm. It was the first time her daughter had raised her voice in such a manner. "Young lady," she said sternly, "I am your mother, and you will *not* speak to me that way. You come out of this car with me right now. We're going inside."

"I hate you!"

"That does it!" Deborah unbuckled her seatbelt and opened the driver's side door. Leaving it open, she walked around to the back, where Rachel was sitting. She opened the door and held it for Rachel. "Let's go!"

Rachel unhooked her lap strap and jumped out, scowling. She stomped her feet all the way to the front door. Her mother was three steps behind her the whole time. When they approached the door, Deborah rang the bell and looked at her daughter.

"Just try to make the best of it, okay?"

Her daughter's eyes were starting to well up with tears. "If you loved me, you wouldn't leave me here."

The words pierced Deborah's heart. But before she could say anything, the door opened. Baylee stood there with her mother.

"Hi, Rachel." Mrs. Marshall smiled warmly.

Deborah looked at her daughter and bent down to give her a hug.

"Don't go, Mommy," Rachel cried in Deborah's arms. "Please."

"I love you," she whispered. She kissed her cheek before letting go and walking away.

The loud engine of the rickety Volvo drowned out some of the noise, but Deborah could still hear Rachel crying. As she got back into the car, she looked up for a moment. Mrs. Marshall and Baylee were both trying to comfort Rachel as she sobbed. It killed her to see her daughter that way.

She backed her car to the bottom of the driveway and shifted the gear into drive. By now, Mrs. Marshall, Baylee and Rachel had disappeared into the house. For a moment, she almost turned the car off. She almost went in to get her daughter. For just a moment, she thought, *Screw it! There'll be other jobs! Go get your baby! Something is wrong!* But she quickly talked herself out of it. *She's just being a child, throwing a fit because she's not getting her way. Mrs. Marshall seems like a lovely lady and she'll take good care of her. Go to work. You need to keep a roof over that child's head.*

She drove on to work and didn't look back.

* * *

Once again, Deborah picked up the phone and dialed Rachel.

After multiple rings, the voicemail message began to play. When she heard the beep at the end, she spoke. "Hey, Rachel, it's Mom. I just wanted to wish you guys a Merry Christmas. Hope you're having a good day. I love you." She hung up the phone and sobbed.

Chapter 24

It was pouring rain the following Tuesday when Daphne arrived at the ACDP meeting. Paul was already there, still saving *two* seats just in case. He turned and smiled at Daphne as she blew through the door. She shook out her umbrella and leaned it against the back wall with several others. She readjusted her shoulder bag and ran her fingers through her hair. Then she clopped in her high-heeled boots all the way over to where Paul was sitting and took the seat beside him.

"Some weather we're having, huh?" He slapped her playfully on the back.

"Ugh, I know! I almost didn't come." She set her bag on her lap and rummaged for her compact. "Just a moment, please." As she checked her makeup and hair, she heard a brief exchange between Paul and another gentleman but never looked up.

"Excuse me," he said to Paul, "is this seat taken."

"Yes, we're saving that for somebody. Sorry."

"No problem." The man walked away and looked for another seat.

Daphne looked at the empty chair and then back at Paul. "Do you think we should keep saving a seat for her? It's been *months*."

He leaned back in his own chair and crossed his arms. "Would you want someone to keep saving the seat for *you*?"

She shrugged. "I guess I would."

"There you go." He winked. "Besides, a promise is a promise. If we can't keep our word, what good are we?"

Not long after that, the meeting started. Ruth stepped up and introduced herself. She welcomed everyone and then proceeded to read a poem that was written by a young woman in the group who had lost her mother. Although she didn't want to be named, she had given Ruth permission to share it at the meeting. She read:

> I was blessed to be your baby
> You carried me in your womb
> You watched me take my first steps
> And taught me to hold a spoon.
>
> I was blessed to be your child
> You came to recitals and plays,
> Concerts and birthday parties
> And you kissed my worries away.
>
> I was blessed to be your teenager
> Through adolescence and acne
> Through dating and disappointment
> You were always there for me.
>
> I was blessed to be your friend
> Once I was fully grown
> You always showed me the glass half full
> And that I never was alone.
>
> I was blessed to be in that room
> The day you took your last breath
> To hold your hand and see your face
> As you crossed from life to death.
>
> I was blessed to be your daughter
> You're with me wherever I roam
> God placed his hand upon you
> And gently carried you home.

Ruth had just finished reading the poem when Paul elbowed Daphne. She looked at him. He turned his head in a way that prompted her to look at the door. Daphne turned. It was Rachel, standing against the back wall.

Without hesitation, Daphne got up and walked to the back to get her. "Hey," she whispered, smiling at Rachel.

"Hey," she whispered back, looking embarrassed.

"Come sit with us," Daphne offered, reaching for her hand.

"Are you sure?"

"Of course." Daphne led the way, and Rachel followed.

They both took their seats. Paul's smile grew when Rachel sat down. He patted her on the knee and whispered, "Welcome back." Rachel gave him a half smile. They all listened quietly to the rest of the meeting. None of them said a word.

Afterward, they all started to get up and stretch.

"Well," said Paul, "it's good to see you again, Rachel."

"Thanks," she said, clearly forcing a smile. "Sorry I haven't been around much. I've just had a lot going on."

Paul waved his hand. "No need to explain, sweetie." He winked. "Well, the wife's got dinner waiting for me, so I'd better scoot. See you all next time."

"Bye," Daphne and Rachel said in unison as they watched him leave.

Through the open door, they could see the sun shining again. The rain had stopped.

"Hey, the rain's cleared up," said Daphne, looking at Rachel. "Do you maybe want to grab a bite somewhere and talk?"

Rachel raised her eyebrows. "Um, sure. I guess. I mean, why not?"

"Great! Is there somewhere nearby that you like to go?"

Rachel grinned. "Yeah, I know a place."

Rachel opened the door of Pete's diner and made sure to hold it for Daphne, who was just behind her.

The same pretty Albanian hostess from the first time she'd been there greeted them cheerfully. "Hi! Table for two?"

"Yes, please," Rachel answered.

Daphne was looking around and smiling.

Rachel followed her new friend's glance to see what was so appealing. When she did, she noticed the quaint décor—floral wallpaper, pictures hanging of the owner's family, and miniature statues of Greek gods. These were things Rachel didn't even see the first time she'd been there. But now, in Daphne's presence, she did.

The seating hostess led them to an empty booth and handed them menus. "Can I get you ladies anything to drink?"

Daphne spoke up first. "Water with lemon, please."

"I'll have the same," said Rachel.

They opened their menus and started to look.

"Wow!" said Daphne. "There are a lot of choices here."

"Yeah, the last time I was here, the cheeseburger was *outstanding*." As soon as Rachel said the words, she blushed and looked down. *She probably doesn't eat that kind of stuff.* "But I think I'd better go healthier this time."

Daphne nodded. "Well, the grilled chicken platter sounds good," she said kindly. "Maybe I'll do rice and kale with that."

What the hell is kale? "Um, that does sound good. I think I'll do the chef salad with reduced-fat ranch."

The hostess came back with two glasses of water and a small bowl filled with lemon wedges. "Here you go, ladies. Sorry for the wait. Our best waitress recently changed to day shift, so the evening service is a little slower."

"No problem," Daphne assured her.

The hostess took their order and then walked away with the menus, leaving them to talk.

"You know," said Rachel, "the last time I was here, I sat at the counter, and the waitress was this pretty young girl with really dark hair, almost black. She seemed like she was sad about something."

"Really?" Daphne said, taking a wedge of lemon and squeezing the juice into her water.

"Yeah." Rachel looked around. "I don't see her tonight, though."

"It's funny how people stick out in our minds like that."

"Oh, I almost forgot," Rachel said, taking out her cell phone. "I'd better text my husband real quick. Excuse me."

She typed: "Grabbing dinner at that little restaurant. Are you guys okay?" She hit Send.

"How long have you been married?" Daphne asked.

"Five years," answered Rachel.

"Nice! Any kids?"

"Yep!" She beamed with pride. "A girl and a boy."

"How old are they?"

The conversation was interrupted by Lee's response.

Rachel apologized and checked it. "Have fun. I'll see you later."

She set the phone aside and changed the subject. "What about you? Are you married?"

Daphne shook her head. "Nope. Love is…sort of complicated for me."

"Why is that?"

"I guess you could say I have abandonment issues. It makes it tough for me to attach fully."

"That's a shame."

Daphne shrugged. "So how did you know that your husband was the one you wanted to marry?"

"Gosh," she said. "No one's ever asked me that before." She pondered for a moment. "I guess you could say he was the only man that ever looked at me, like I was already the person that I *wanted* to be…if that makes any sense at all."

"Actually," Daphne smiled, "it makes *perfect* sense."

* * *

It was about seven thirty when Rachel walked through the door at home. She left her shoes in the entryway and followed the sound of Lee's voice into the living room. Both Avery and Nick were bathed and in PJs, cuddled on the couch, while Lee read them a bedtime story.

Avery saw Rachel first. "Hi, Mommy," she said sweetly as she climbed off the couch and ran to her. Rachel scooped her up in her arms and hugged her tightly. She kissed the top of her head ten times before putting her down. Avery grabbed her hand and started leading her toward the couch. "Come here, Mommy. I'll sit in your lap, and Nick can have Daddy's."

Rachel and Lee both chuckled. She sat down beside him and leaned in for a kiss. He gave her a peck on the lips. "Did you have fun?"

She sighed. "Yes, I did, actually. In fact, I'd like to do it again in two weeks, if that's cool."

"Sure." He nodded. "Why not next week, though?"

"She's going to be out of town."

"Ah." He smiled and turned the page of the book to read more.

"Hey, Lee?" she said.

"What?"

"I think we should start taking walks together as a family. You know, like before dinner when it's still light out. Maybe we could start tomorrow?"

He kissed her forehead. "Consider it done."

Chapter 25

It was a Sunday afternoon. Kate had the day off, and the weather was just cold enough for sweatpants and a hoodie. She stretched out on the couch to watch TV. After channel-surfing for a bit, she found an old black-and-white film. *Yes! I love this one.* Twenty minutes into the movie, she had drifted off to sleep.

And as Kate slept, she dreamed…

There was water all around her. At first, she thought she was fully submerged in the ocean. Then she realized she was completely dry. Bubbles encircled her, clouding her vision. She could barely make out the large figure before her. It was a bluish-gray blob floating gracefully on the water.

She began to realize she was not in the ocean. In fact, she wasn't outside at all. She was indoors. It was an aquarium. Kate was on her second-grade class field trip. Gradually, it became clear. She was dreaming about something that had actually happened.

Kate looked over her shoulder to see other children walking around and marveling at the other sea creatures. Her teacher, Ms. Frances, sauntered up and knelt down beside her.

"Do you know what kind of animal this is?" she asked Kate, touching the glass with her index finger.

Kate had been glued to it for several minutes, unable to pull herself away.

She took a closer look at the sea creature and saw its round head, sunken eyes, and eight long tentacles. "An octopus?" She turned to her teacher.

"Right!" Her teacher beamed proudly. "And we learned that there are two things that make an octopus really special. Do you remember?"

Young Kate looked at the octopus again, who seemed to be looking straight back at her. "It has three hearts?"

"That's right!" Once again, Ms. Frances was pleased by the child's recitation. "And what else makes it so special?"

Suddenly, Kate woke up. There were footsteps gently making their way up the front steps of the house, followed by a soft knock on the door. She reached for her cell phone on the coffee table to check the time.

It's 5:00 p.m. That'll be Elizabeth. Same time as usual.

She sat up, propping herself on one elbow, and looked at the door. The outline of Elizabeth's body could be seen through the curtain. She waited patiently for almost a minute. When it became apparent that Kate was not coming to the door, she bent down for a moment and then stood back up. She turned around and walked away.

Kate made sure to allot enough time for Elizabeth to be out of sight before getting up off the couch. She swung her legs around slowly and let her bare feet touch the cool hardwood floor. She stretched her arms over her head briefly. Then she pushed away from the couch and came up to a standing position slowly and carefully. Each step she took toward the door made the old wooden floorboards squeak.

When she opened the door, she found a casserole dish covered in tin foil. She bent down and picked it up carefully. It was still warm. The smell made her mouth water. She brought it inside and made sure the door was locked before taking the food into the kitchen.

She laid the dish on the counter and slowly peeled back the foil, letting the small drops of condensation drip. *Spinach pie.* The aroma tickled the inside of her nose. *Mmm, Elizabeth never disappoints.*

Immediately, she took out a plate and a spatula and served herself a piece. Then she poured a glass of water and sat at the kitchen counter alone. As she took her first bite, she got up for a moment and grabbed her cell phone from the coffee table. She checked it for messages, but there were none.

He's not gonna call, Kate. You're gonna have to make the next move.

I will. Just not today.

When is it ever a good day? This baby is going to be here before you know it. He has a right to be involved.

Annoyed, she dropped her fork and reached for her cell phone. She selected Adam's number and was about to hit Call. She stared at the phone like she'd stared at the octopus in her dream.

What are you waiting for? She set the phone on the counter, facing upward. Her finger hovered over the green button as she continued to devour her meal with her free hand. When she had finished eating, she exited Call Mode on her phone. Then she went back for another slice of Elizabeth's spinach pie.

Chapter 26

The pilot's voice came over the intercom. "Ladies and gentleman, we're about to begin our descent into Tucson International Airport. The current temperature is fifty-eight degrees with clear skies. It's a beautiful day in Arizona. Approximate arrival time will be 3:20 p.m. Please make sure you're seated with your seat belts securely fastened, tray tables should be closed, and seat backs should be in their upright positions. Thank you for flying with us today....and I'll see you on the ground."

Daphne closed the book that she'd been reading. She reached under the seat in front of her for her handbag, shoved the novel inside carelessly, and pushed the bag back under the seat with her foot. Sitting up straight again, she breathed deeply and shut her eyes.

Relax...it'll be over soon. Just breathe and relax.

After a few minutes, the pressure change started to make her feel nauseated. She leaned forward again and reached for her purse. She opened the inner zip pouch and pulled out her emergency stash of baby wipes. Hastily, she pulled one out and rubbed it on the back of her neck. The nausea slowly began to subside. She continued to breathe deeply and pressed the cool wipe to her left ear and then the right one.

Almost there. It's gonna be fine.

She looked out the window to get an idea of how close they were to the ground. There were no more clouds in sight, and the buildings and houses looked like miniature models on a game board.

Not much longer...keep breathing.

Daphne stuck the bag of wipes back in her purse and quickly slid it under the seat once more. She leaned forward and looked out the window again. They were moments from touching the runway.

She sat back and closed her eyes. *It's just like a basketball bouncing. Be the ball.*

The airplane bounced once, projecting them back into the air for a second. Then twice and a third time almost instantly…until the aircraft was gliding along the runway smoothly. Some of the passengers clapped. Daphne opened her eyes and exhaled loudly. She waited patiently for the plane to stop before grabbing her purse and standing up to exit the plane.

Once she retrieved her overnight bag and left the plane, it was just a hop, a skip, and a jump to the car rental area. She had paid extra to ensure that all she had to do was go out to the parking lot and locate her assigned vehicle. She looked at the reservation information on her phone to confirm that she had the right car—a green Toyota Corolla. The car was already unlocked, and the keys were in the visor. She threw her overnight bag into the back seat and placed the key in the ignition. As she turned it, the intensity of the AC and the volume of the music startled her. She turned both down and reached for her phone again to open the Maps app.

"Holy Trinity," she typed into the search box. The giant circle in the middle of the phone spun for a few seconds before pulling up the results…Holy Trinity Catholic Church.

That's got to be it.

She tapped the address to see how far it was from her present location.

Forty-three minutes. Okay. Let's do this.

She selected Navigation Mode on her Maps app and started following its directions. After a maze of twists, turns, and ridiculous maneuvers, she finally found herself on the freeway, ready to drive straight for several miles. She turned on the satellite radio and scrolled for a song that fit her mood. It didn't take long, however, before her thoughts started trumping the sound of the music.

This is crazy. I shouldn't be here. This is crazy. What if she's not there? What if it's the wrong church. I'm flying back tomorrow, so I don't have much time. This is crazy!

The navigation voice alerted her that a turn was coming in one mile. She checked her mirror and then over her shoulder to make sure she could get into the right lane. It was all clear.

She signaled and changed lanes. She turned the music off so that she could focus. The voice continued to direct her through various turns until at last she saw the old but elegant church coming up on the right. Her heart became heavy. Her mouth went dry. She slowed the car down and eased into a parking space on the street.

For a moment, she sat in the car, staring at the church. She listened to the soft hum of the engine.

You started this, Daphne. See it through.

She turned the car off and made sure there was no oncoming traffic before opening the door. As she slowly walked along the cobblestones leading up to the church, she felt a sudden rush of déjà vu.

Have I been here before? Did I dream about it? Maybe it's just wishful thinking.

Her hands began to shake. She found herself standing in front of two large wooden double doors with oversized knockers. Above each knocker was a Christmas wreath with a large red bow. She gently pushed on the right-side door. It creaked loudly as it opened.

Inside, it was dark and at least ten degrees cooler. Daphne stepped in quietly and wrapped her sweater around herself tightly. The organist was practicing, filling the church with the melody of "How Great Thou Art." The icicle lights from Christmas were still decorating the entrance. The statue of Jesus dying on the cross humbled Daphne.

She took a few more steps and noticed a hallway with opened doors all in a row.

Maybe one of these is Sister Angelina's office.

She turned and started walking down the hall to investigate. No sooner than she'd turned the corner there was a voice behind her.

"Can I help you?" a woman's voice asked kindly.

Daphne turned to see a middle-aged woman dressed in complete nun attire. She even wore a habit, hiding her hair. She was smiling and holding a stack of hymn books.

"Yes, hello," she stammered. "Um, I'm looking for Sister Angelina"

The nun looked surprised. "Oh, I see. Ah, what's your name, dear?"

"Daphne," she said, extending her hand. "Daphne Weavers."

"Hi, Daphne." She shook her hand. "I'm Sister Claire. Could we step into my office? It's just this first door on the right."

"Sure," she answered, following Sister Claire.

Sister Claire placed the hymn books on top of her desk. "Please have a seat." She motioned toward a chair near the door, opposite her own chair behind the desk. "Can I get you any coffee or tea?"

"Oh no, thank you." Daphne sat down.

"Where are you from, Daphne."

"Florida."

Sister Claire's eyes widened. "Then you've come a long way."

"Yes, I flew in just this afternoon and came straight here."

Sister Claire smiled. "Well, I suppose I can guess why you're here then."

Daphne raised her eyebrows.

"You're one of them."

"Sorry, one of w*hom*?"

"You're one of the children."

Daphne felt a sudden chill.

"Many years ago, someone abandoned a newborn baby on the front steps of this church. Sister Angelina immediately took to the child and wanted to take care of her. So she elected herself the baby's guardian until she was able to find a suitable home for her."

"Wow," Daphne sighed.

"But it didn't end there. Once word got out in the community about what Sister Angelina had done, this became a popular place for unwed mothers to leave their children."

"That's so sad. How many children were left here?"

Sister Claire thought for a moment. "Hmm, I'd say at least a dozen. Well, over the course of several years, that is."

"Still," Daphne said in shock, "that's an awful lot of unwanted children."

"Well, perhaps *unwanted* is the wrong term. Maybe *awaiting their true parents* is a more appropriate phrase."

Daphne half-smiled.

"I think Sister Angelina and I can help you. Would you like to meet her?"

"Oh yes, please!"

"Follow me, dear." She stood up and headed toward the back of the church through the sanctuary. On the way, they walked right past the organist and exchanged nods. Sister Claire held the door open for Daphne. "Watch your step."

She looked down and stepped onto another cobblestone path. They entered a beautiful garden with flowers, trees, and fountains. Daphne breathed in the refreshing, botanical scent.

"We have to go through the garden to get to her, dear."

Daphne followed without saying a word. She was mesmerized by the natural beauty that surrounded her. As they continued walking, she noticed that there was a cemetery in another part of the garden. There were headstones up and down the edge of the walkway. There was a small house at the end of the trail. "Oh, is that where she is?" Daphne pointed to the house.

Sister Claire suddenly stopped in front of one of the headstones. Daphne knelt down and looked closely. Her heart sank.

Sister Angelina O'Brien
Beloved daughter of God
who brought hope
to countless others

"Not anymore," replied Sister Claire.

Chapter 27

While Daphne was in Tucson, learning about Sister Angelina's demise, Rachel was arriving at her psychologist's office.

Dr. Nova welcomed her with a smile. "Rachel, I'm so glad you came back."

Rachel smiled back and stepped inside. "How are you?"

"Oh, fine," she answered and closed the door. "I wasn't sure I'd hear from you after our last session."

Rachel was standing next to the piano in the sitting room outside the office. "I…guess I just wasn't ready that day."

"Well, let's chat." She motioned for Rachel to follow her and walked into the office.

They sat down and made themselves comfortable. Rachel held on to her purse for the moment.

"So," Dr. Nova sighed, "talk to me. What made you want to come back today?"

Rachel gulped. "I…think I'm ready to deal with what happened after my dad died. I need to figure out a way to forgive and move past it."

Dr. Nova nodded. "You deserve that."

Rachel reached into her purse and pulled out the infamous necklace. She held it up for Dr. Nova to see. "My daughter found this recently."

The doctor squinted. "I don't think I've seen that before. What is that?"

Rachel clasped it in her hand like a fragile egg. "It's my half of a pair of 'BEST FRIENDS' charms......Baylee gave it to me. She wore the other half."

Dr. Nova's eyes widened. "She *did*?"

"Right after she made me promise to keep what happened to us a secret." Rachel nodded. Her nose began to itch.

"Rachel, you've been carrying that necklace for all of these years, just like you've been carrying the emotion inside you...the anger, the pain, the guilt..."

Her head was down. Tears began to form.

"Are you angry with Baylee?"

"I *was* at first." She looked up. "When she first asked me to keep the secret, I *hated* her."

"When did that change?"

Rachel laughed through her tears. "The same day!"

"*Why* did your feelings change?"

"Because I looked in her eyes and realized we were in the same boat, the same secret, the same fears... I think she felt like her hands were tied, and I couldn't untie them for her."

"Are you mad at yourself for that?"

The tears intensified. "*I* got away... *She* didn't! I only had to endure that for one summer! The next year, we moved away. We got into an apartment. I went to another school, and they had summer day camp. I never had to go back after that, but she *stayed*. And God knows how much worse it got!"

"But don't you see? You *didn't* leave her. You've *always* been locked in with her. That's what that necklace *represents*—your unwillingness to let her go!"

Rachel's eyes widened—the tears made them sparkle like glass. She looked down at the piece of jewelry. Her hand shook. "I couldn't save her, just like I couldn't save my dad, and I *hate that* about myself!"

Dr. Nova leaned back in her chair and looked pensive. "Why did you have children, Rachel?"

"What does that have to do with it?" she asked, looking annoyed.

"A lot, actually."

Rachel sighed and thought for a minute. "I guess I had a lot of love to give."

"I'm sure that's true," the doctor said. "But why else? Think about it."

She pictured Avery's face…and then Nick's. She thought about the joy that filled her heart whenever she heard either one of them laughing. She thought about the pain she endured whenever one of them cried. Then she thought about the fire inside of her that would surely be ignited if anyone ever entertained the notion of harming them the way she'd been harmed. It would be enough for her to want to kill. Suddenly, it was clear. "I wanted to give them what *I* wasn't given."

Dr. Nova smiled proudly. "Go on."

"I wanted to have children so that I could protect them the way children deserve to be protected. I wanted to listen to them when they need to be heard and love them and make them feel secure…because I didn't have that." Her head dropped again. "I guess I thought that if I could do that for at least one child, it might start to make up for *my* pain."

The doctor tipped her head, trying to get Rachel to raise hers. "Has that worked?"

"Maybe a little, I guess." She shrugged. The image of Avery's sad face after she'd been playing with Baylee's necklace haunted her. "But I'm not perfect."

"No one is, Rachel."

"I know that." She finally looked up. "But if my failure to overcome this gets in the way of being the kind of mom I want to be, well, that's just unacceptable."

Dr. Nova said nothing. She just listened.

Rachel looked at Dr. Nova and swallowed. "So where do I go from here?"

She looked at her watch. "Well, we're out of time for today. I think we'd better tackle this in another session. Can you come back next Tuesday? Same time?"

"Can we make it earlier, please? I have somewhere to be at four thirty."

Chapter 28

D aphne and Sister Claire had just reentered the church. They walked somberly side by side through the sanctuary.

"I don't understand, Sister Claire. When we spoke earlier, you said that you *and* Sister Angelina could help me. How can she help if she's no longer alive?"

Sister Claire stopped in the middle of the aisle and smiled. "There is much you don't know about life and death."

Daphne sighed impatiently. *Be nice. She's a nun, and she wants to help.*

"When we die, sometimes we leave things behind that allow us to live on and fulfill our purpose, even from beyond. Sister Angelina was a very wise woman. She knew someday each of the children being left here would want to know where they came from. But without a proper birth certificate, that would be difficult. So she created the next best thing."

"What was that?" Daphne asked anxiously.

"Follow me," Sister Claire commanded. She turned and headed back toward the hallway of offices, past her own, and down to the very end of the hall. There was a storage closet. She opened it to reveal a file cabinet. "In what year were you born?"

Daphne inched closer, squinting to see the tiny labels that had been placed on each drawer: 1979–1989, 1990–2000, 2000–present. Her heart started pounding. "First drawer. 1980."

Sister Claire opened the top drawer carefully, ensuring that nothing slid out of place or became wrinkled. Gently, she thumbed through the file tags one by one. "Here it is. What month?"

"April," Daphne answered. She could feel her temple throbbing. Sweat began to form under her arms.

Sister Claire reached in and pulled out a file marked April 1980. "This is the only one there." She held it out for Daphne.

This is it. If you grab that file and look inside, that's it. No turning back. She reached up slowly and took it. "Thank you, Sister Claire." It felt light, almost as if there was nothing inside. Then she opened it. There was a picture of a newborn baby swaddled in a blanket inside a small cardboard box. The baby's eyes were closed. She was resting peacefully, unaware of her surroundings. Her tiny fingers were spread over her cheeks. There was no cap on her head to keep her warm.

Daphne flipped the picture over to the back and began to cry. It said: April 4, 1980. "Are you sure this is the only one?"

"Yes, dear," answered Sister Claire. "She was very careful with her files."

Daphne stared at the picture in disbelief. "So...*this* is how my life began?"

"Why don't you sit down, Daphne?" Sister Claire tried to lead her back to her office, but Daphne just sat on the carpet right there with her back against the wall.

"How could somebody *do* that?" Daphne said angrily. "How do you take a newborn baby that you just gave birth to...and stick her in a *box*...and just leave?" Tears poured down her face.

"Daphne," Sister Claire knelt down beside her and rubbed her back. "Please try not to be angry with your mother. You don't know what she was going through or what prompted her to do what she did. It's important to remember that no matter how she did it, she gave you life. Isn't that what counts?"

She wiped her tears and showed Sister Claire the picture. "Whatever it was, it must have been pretty bad to do *that* to a baby! Forgive me, Sister Claire. Maybe I can forgive her one day but *not* today. I need a moment to let this sink in before I can even *begin* to think about that."

"Of course you do," the nun said tenderly.

119

Daphne sighed. "So this is where it ends, huh? No address. No information. Just a picture of an abandoned baby who happens to be me?"

Sister Claire nodded sympathetically. "I know it's of little comfort, dear, but you're welcome to take the picture with you."

She slowly turned her head to face her. "What for?"

Sister Claire placed her hand on top of Daphne's. "Believe me, it might come in handy one day." With that, she stood up and offered her hand to help Daphne onto her feet.

* * *

Later that night, in the darkness of the hotel room, Daphne lay restless. She'd taken a sleep aid thirty minutes before turning out the lights. Yet it didn't seem to have any effect. She was haunted by the picture that was now tucked in her overnight bag. She couldn't shake off the anger over how her mother had disposed of her, and she was even more angry at the thought that her search had hit a dead end.

This can't be the end, damn it! It just can't!

There's nothing you can do about it. Let it go.

I can't! I don't accept that!

She began thinking about what Ray, the professor, had talked about the night he spoke at the ACDP meeting. It was the same concept Renee had described when she talked about being in the hospital and tuning into the sounds around her. Daphne wondered, could she, too, learn this trick of peeling back the layers of noise and truly hear the silence?

She got very quiet. Anytime a thought began to creep its way in, she blocked it out by tuning in to the subtle sounds in the room, like the air conditioner. She closed her eyes and listened deeper. The faucet in the bathroom had a quiet drip that occurred about every ten seconds. She kept listening and heard the hum of the ice machine in the hallway outside her room.

She waited and listened. Pretty soon the world was quiet—truly quiet. She could feel her typical negative thoughts begin pushing through again, and again she ignored them.

Suddenly, a new voice emerged. Daphne couldn't really hear the words out loud, as they were coming from inside her—inside her mind. From a place she didn't even know existed. *Don't think*, it said. *Just listen.*

More silence.

Then just before she drifted off to sleep, the answer came to her. *Of course! She was right. Sister Angelina was a wise woman.*

Daphne drifted off to sleep peacefully, knowing exactly what she had to do the next day.

Chapter 29

Kate had worked the midday shift and was home by 6:00 p.m. She showered, put on her warm pajamas, and ate dinner in the living room while watching TV. Her meal consisted of macaroni and cheese with a side of steamed broccoli and a glass of 1 percent milk.

When she finished dinner, she cleaned up the kitchen, loaded the dishwasher, and wiped down the counter. Then she put the tray table in the corner of the living room where she usually kept it and stretched out on the couch. Her eyelids became increasingly heavy. By eight o'clock, she was just about asleep. Suddenly, she got a text. Kate grabbed her phone and read the message. It was from Adam.

"Is it okay if I come over?"

It's him! Oh my gosh, I'm not ready.

You can't avoid him forever.

Ugh!

She texted back: "Okay." Her heart began beating a mile a minute.

Less than five minutes later, there was a knock on the door that startled Kate. *Could that be him already?* She checked the peephole to make sure. There he was, wearing a black-and-white checked hoodie. His hands were in his pockets, and he was shivering from the cold. Kate unlocked the deadbolt and opened the door.

"That was quick," she said, still in shock.

"I've been across the street for about an hour," Adam responded. He stepped into the house and stood next to the bench, turning to face her again. "I wasn't sure if I should come over or not."

Kate shut the door and locked it. "You were over there for *an hour?*"

He looked away. "I do that every Tuesday."

Her eyes widened in disbelief.

"Well, maybe not for an hour necessarily but every Tuesday, yes."

"Do you want to sit down?" she offered, pointing toward the living room.

"Sure," he answered. He took his hoodie off and hung it on the coat rack. He also removed his shoes and placed them beside the bench.

Kate sat in an armchair.

Adam followed her in and sat on the couch.

"I wanted to wait long enough," he said, "until you could decide what you're going to do."

She shrugged. "I'm *having* a baby, Adam. That's all I know."

"So...are you thinking of *keeping* it, or are you thinking *adoption?*"

Kate leaned back in her chair and brought her legs up, sitting Indian-style. "I wish I knew."

Adam noticed her pregnancy bump for the first time. A lump formed in his throat. He swallowed as hard as he could.

"I...don't know if I have what it takes to be a mom."

He listened quietly. His face didn't reveal any emotion.

"On the other hand," she continued, "how do I grow a human being inside me and then just let it go?"

"Kate, I think I'm in love with you," Adam blurted out.

Oh, God. Please don't say that.

"I know my timing sucks, but I can't go on *not* saying it."

She cleared her throat. "Are you just saying this to try to convince me to keep her?"

"*Her?*" His face lit up.

"I-I don't know yet. It's just a feeling I have."

He nodded, appearing a bit disappointed. "Well, to answer your question, no. I don't know what we should do about the baby, but this is something I've felt for a long time."

"How long are we talking?"

"Like, since *always*."

"*Always?*" she asked. "Like since we were *kids*?"

He nodded again.

"Adam," she said sadly. "You don't even *know* me. You didn't know me *then* either."

"Maybe you're right," he agreed. "All I know is that the first day you walked into my classroom in second grade, I couldn't stop looking at you. Anytime you looked down to do your work, my eyes were on you. When you were absent for days at a time, I couldn't stop wondering where you were. And when you came back, it was like the first day of school all over again. At the beginning of every new year, I'd hold my breath, waiting to see if you'd show up…until our senior year when you just disappeared altogether."

Kate looked down.

"There hasn't been a day since then that I haven't thought of you. And then when I saw you again, it was like a part of me that had died came back to life."

Tears welled up in her eyes.

"Then we spent the night together, and it was the best night of my *life*. And then to find out that that night created a *new life…*"

Finally, Kate looked up again. Her cheeks were stained with tears, and her eyes were red. "Like I said, I don't know what it takes to be a mom. I don't remember my mom."

"Kate, what happened to you?"

She stood up and went to the kitchen counter, where she kept a box of tissues. She wiped her tears and blew her nose. Then she threw the wadded-up tissue into the trash can at the end of the counter. She cleaned her hands with sanitizer and returned to her chair. "My parents…" She paused and shut her eyes tightly. She breathed in for four seconds and out for four through her nose. She opened her eyes and sat in the armchair again. "My parents died in a car accident when I was a toddler."

Adam's eyes sank. "I'm sorry, Kate."

"They never assigned a legal guardian, so I became a ward of the state." She shrugged.

"Wasn't there a relative or a friend? Somebody that could step up and take care of you?"

Kate threw her hands up. "Apparently not. I've asked myself that a hundred times."

"So you were in foster care."

She nodded abruptly. "And not the good kind either. Oh, and by the way, when I missed school for days at a stretch, that was probably because I was hiding out and waiting for my bruises to heal before anyone at school could see them."

Adam opened his mouth, as if he was about to speak, but nothing came out.

"And you know, I always used to say to myself that if I was the perfect child—well-behaved, kept everything clean, didn't talk back—maybe I wouldn't get shuffled around from home to home so much. Or at least end up someplace where I didn't get the crap kicked out of me."

Adam's hands shook. He looked like he wanted to punch a hole through a wall.

"It's okay, Adam. It stopped, eventually. And hey, I learned how to keep things spotless, so it wasn't for nothing."

He slowly dropped to his knees and crawled over to the chair where she was sitting. He kneeled in front of her. "What can I do?"

She shook her head and started crying again. "I don't know."

He wrapped his arms around her and held her. "It's okay. You don't have to tell me anything else. Just let me be here for you... please."

Kate started to place her head on his shoulder but quickly pulled away. "I don't want to mess up your shirt."

He cradled her face between his hands. "Kate, it's *okay*. Forget the shirt. It's *fine*."

She finally gave in. She rested her head on Adam's shoulder and cried until she was too exhausted to cry any more.

When Kate was done, Adam helped her up slowly. He led her to the bedroom and made sure she was warm and comfortable in her bed. Then he shut the door and went to sleep on the couch.

Chapter 30

As soon as Daphne's plane hit the ground in Florida, she was the first one up out of her seat to grab her carry-on bag from the overhead compartment. With her luggage in tow, she nearly knocked over the flight attendant standing at the entryway of the cockpit. "Sorry!" she yelled as she stepped off the plane. "Thank you! Have a nice day!"

That was rude, Daphne.

Shut up! We're on a mission.

She whipped out the ticket stub from the day before and power walked all the way to the elevators that led to the parking garage. She pushed the Down button, and nothing lit up for several seconds.

Ugh! Mother!

Bing! One of the elevators chimed. Its doors opened. She waited impatiently for a family of five to vacate the elevator. Once it was clear, she stepped in and immediately pushed the button for the level where her car was waiting. To her delight, no one else stepped onto the elevator.

When the elevator doors opened again, she resumed power walking all the way to her car, popped the trunk open, and was about to throw her carry-on bag in hastily.

Be careful. There's precious cargo in there.

She closed the trunk and unlocked the car doors. Gently, she placed the small suitcase on the floor of the back seat and shut the door. Then she began her route home, one that included a stop at the pharmacy.

Daphne burst through the automatic double doors like a cyborg. Her only acknowledgment of the employee that welcomed her on the way in was a quick wave. There was simply no time for pleasantries. She grabbed a shopping basket and headed for the office supply section.

Jumbo-sized index cards...Sharpees... She snatched the items and dropped them into her basket. *Done.*

She strutted to the checkout line. There was only one lane open, and another customer was completing her purchase. She was also wasting time making small talk with the cashier. Daphne's eyes moved from left to right, looking at the candy strategically placed for impulse buying. Her stomach growled.

Suddenly, the cashier looked at her. "Are you ready, ma'am?"

"Yes," Daphne replied. She quickly stepped up and placed her items on the counter.

"How are you today?" she asked.

"Good," said Daphne without looking up. She was busily fishing out her credit card. "How about you?"

"No complaints," said the cashier.

There was no further conversation until the cashier handed Daphne her receipt.

"Have a nice day," she said.

Daphne took the receipt and shoved it in the bag with the Sharpees and index cards. "Thanks. You too," she said, as if the three words had morphed into one. Before she knew it, she was out the door and in her car. It was only a three-minute drive from the pharmacy to her apartment.

I can't believe I'm actually doing this. It's kind of stupid.

People have done it before.

Yeah, and I thought they were stupid.

Well, what other options do you have?

None, I guess.

So we're doing this!

As soon as Daphne got into her apartment, she slipped off her boots and tossed them in the foyer with the countless other shoes that waited to be put away in the closet properly. She dashed to her bedroom and put her suitcase on her bed.

I'll unpack later.

Carefully but eagerly, she pulled out the picture that Sister Claire gave her and carried it to the dining room table. Next, she reached for the pharmacy bag and took out the index cards and Sharpees. She got right to work.

When she felt like the cards looked just right, she went to the bathroom mirror to ensure that she looked presentable, at least from the neck up. She touched up her makeup and took extended time straightening and shaping her hair. After that, she went back to the dining room, pulled out her iPad, and opened the video app. Then she turned the camera toward herself.

Ugh! This light is too bright.

She adjusted it and looked again.

This shirt is all wrong. The red washes me out. Maybe something blue.

She changed her shirt and looked again.

Hmm, I guess this'll work. All right, here goes everything.

She took a deep breath and hit Record.

* * *

A few hours later, Avery and Nick were down for the night. Rachel and Lee were in the living room about to enjoy some relaxation. Rachel grabbed her iPad to check her social media account and saw that she had a notification: "Daphne Weavers tagged you on a new video."

Hmm, I wonder what that's about.

The caption read: "Please share this with as many people as you can."

Rachel hit Play and watched.

Daphne was in her dining room. She was completely silent. To communicate, she held up a series of pre-written messages on index cards. They read as follows:

Hi. My name is Daphne... I was born on April 4, 1980...I think... See, I was left at a church when I was a newborn... This is my picture.

In the video, Daphne held up the baby picture with her left hand and kept it there while she continued flipping the message cards with her right hand.

If enough people share this video, eventually it might reach my birth mother... If it does, please know I'm looking for you... I don't want anything from you... I just want to meet you... Thank you... Please share.

"What's up?" Lee asked from his corner of the couch.

Rachel hadn't realized that her jaw was hanging open. "It's just this video that Daphne posted on Facebook."

"Is that your friend from ACDP? The one you had dinner with?"

"Uh-huh."

"What kind of video?"

Rachel sighed. "She's trying to find her birth mother."

Without hesitation, she forwarded the message to everyone in her contacts list.

Chapter 31

I t was six o'clock in the morning, and Rachel was up before the kids, to get ready for the day. She had showered, blow-dried her hair, and thrown it up into her typical messy bun. She applied a thin layer of mineral foundation and just a touch of eye shadow. She caught a quick glimpse of herself in the mirror and examined her figure carefully. *Hmm, the love handles seem to be getting smaller. Still there, though. Got to keep working at it.*

Then she moved over to the dresser that was against the wall between the bathroom door and the bed where Lee was lying asleep. She opened the top drawer for a pair of socks. As she closed the drawer again, the light coming in from the bathroom shone on her jewelry box. Rachel thought about Baylee's necklace, which was tucked away neatly inside. Her heart thumped. She opened the jewelry box and took it out, remembering the day she'd been given the necklace. It was the day she found out why Baylee was afraid of her father.

* * *

Seven-year-old Rachel came out of the Marshalls' house through the back door, shaking with fright. *Where is Baylee?*

She wandered around the backyard aimlessly for a minute. The grass and trees behind the house suddenly looked a putrid shade of green, not bright and vibrant like they had appeared that morning. The sky looked gray and ugly. Even the butterflies that usually fluttered about playfully seemed to have disappeared.

She must be in her hiding place. Rachel turned and walked toward the back deck. She crouched and peeked underneath. Sure enough, there she was, huddled in the dirt, hugging her knees and rocking gently back and forth.

Slowly, Rachel got on her hands and knees and crawled beneath the deck to where Baylee was. She sat down beside her. Neither one said a word at first. They could barely look at each other.

"Did he?" Baylee asked.

Rachel nodded and then lowered her head.

Baylee nodded back. "I'm sorry."

"Why didn't you tell me?" she asked angrily but quietly.

Baylee buried her face in her knees. "He said if I told anybody, he was going to hurt me."

"He told me the same thing," she said in a weak voice.

They both cried softly.

"What are we going to do, Baylee? I'm scared."

"Don't be scared." She placed a hand on Rachel's shoulder.

Rachel flinched.

Baylee backed off. "It'll be okay. We just have to keep it a secret."

"My mom told me that some things shouldn't be kept a secret. We should tell another adult."

Baylee's eyes filled with terror. "No! Don't tell anyone, Rachel. It'll be okay. I promise."

Rachel cringed.

"How about if I give you one of these?" She placed her hand on the gold chain she always wore, the one with the two pendants spelling out "BEST FRIENDS."

Rachel just stared at them for a moment.

"Best friends share secrets, right? And they do things for each other."

Rachel nodded.

"So let's be best friends. You'll never tell and I'll never tell. Everything will be okay."

Rachel wanted to throw up. She wanted to say no and was angry that Baylee would even suggest such a thing.

"Please, Rachel," Baylee begged, looking petrified.

Rachel began to realize that she may not have a choice. If she went home and told her mother, she'd probably call Baylee's mother. Baylee would deny it, and both of their moms would think she was a liar. They'd be mad at her. Baylee would stop being her friend. It would just make everything worse. "Okay," she finally answered with a lump in her throat.

Baylee smiled. She unfastened the chain in the back, removed it, and placed it in the dirt. Carefully, she slipped off the charm that said "ST ENDS" and handed it to Rachel.

Rachel reluctantly took it in the palm of her hand and made a fist. She looked at Baylee and smiled as bravely as she could.

"Best friends," said Baylee.

* * *

Lee woke up and saw Rachel standing at the dresser, staring at the necklace. "Hey," he said quietly.

Once Rachel heard him, she came back to the present. She took a deep breath. "Hey."

"Are you okay?" he asked.

"Uh-huh."

He got out of bed and stood beside her. "What are you thinking about?"

She showed him the necklace cupped in her hand. "This."

Lee looked at it and then at her but said nothing.

"I know I should have gotten rid of it a long time ago."

"Better late than never," he said, squeezing her shoulders.

She swallowed. "I want to. I *really* do."

"You know, you're always saying that everything happens for a reason. So maybe there's a reason why Avery found that necklace. Maybe it was to show you that you still have some healing to do."

Rachel nodded. "You're right. I know you're right. It's definitely time. I'm just not sure how to go about it."

"Isn't that what Dr. Nova is for?"

"True, but ultimately, I have to be willing to follow through on her advice."

"Would you like to hear *my* advice?"

"Sure." She turned toward him.

He looked deep into her eyes. "Just do it."

Rachel raised her eyebrows. "That's all you've got?"

"I know it sounds like I'm downplaying it, but seriously, *just do it*. Drop it in the toilet...or the trash...or into a body of water somewhere." He took the necklace from her and squeezed it in his fist. "This damned thing is like an *anchor*. It's keeping you stuck in the same spot. You don't need to keep punishing yourself. I mean, haven't you suffered enough?"

Rachel sighed. "It's like the chicken and the egg, you know?"

"What do you mean?" he asked, furrowing his brow.

"I don't know what comes first. Do I have to build up the confidence to get rid of it first? Or do I get rid of it now, hoping that I'll *become* ready."

Lee smiled. "There are some things in life that we can't prepare for, Rachel. Like I said, just do it."

Chapter 32

Kate was wiping down the counter at the diner. It had been weeks since her last face-to-face conversation with Adam. And yet she couldn't stop thinking about him. She kept remembering over and over again how her heart had leapt when she got up the next day and saw him sleeping on her couch. The image of his face as he lay there sleeping was burned into her memory. She probably would have watched him sleep longer if it hadn't been for the squeaky floorboard that she'd stepped on.

* * *

The noise had startled Adam and awakened him. He looked around the living room, trying to recall where he was.

"Hey," Kate had said softly, stepping closer to him as quietly as she could.

"Hey," he replied as he began to get up and stretch. "Um, you were so tired last night. I didn't want to make you get out of bed to lock the door behind me, so I just crashed. I hope that's okay."

She nodded. "Thanks. Do you want some coffee...or some breakfast?"

"I'm okay," he assured her, walking toward the entryway. He sat on the wooden bench and started putting on his shoes.

Kate sat on the arm of the couch, facing him. "So where do we go from here?"

Adam stopped tying his shoe for a moment. "Wherever you want, I guess."

"What if I don't know what I want?"

He finished tying his shoes and stood up. He looked at her, sitting in the living room, shook his head, and smiled.

"What?" She smiled back.

"This." He pointed to her, then to himself, and then back at her. "This is sort of our dynamic right now, isn't it?"

"What do you mean?"

"I mean"—he pointed to the hardwood floor beneath his feet—"I know this is always where you take your shoes off, and if I come over there right now to where you are, I'd be crossing a line that makes you uncomfortable. So you're over there on your side, and I'm over here on mine, and I can't get to you."

* * *

"Excuse me, Miss?" a man's voice came from a nearby booth.

Kate looked up and saw a middle-aged man with glasses. He looked familiar, but she couldn't quite remember where she'd seen him before. She walked over to his booth. "Yes, sir," she said. "I'm sorry. How can I help you?"

"Could I please get a refill on my coffee?" he asked politely.

"Sure." She went to the kitchen for a fresh pot and came back to his booth.

"You look familiar," he said as she filled his cup. "Maybe you've waited on me before?"

She looked at him more closely. Suddenly, she remembered. "Oh, I know. You were a speaker one night at an ACDP meeting a few months ago. You're a professor. I was in the audience that night."

He snapped his fingers. "That's it."

"Is there anything else I can get you right now?"

"No, thank you." He reached for a pack of sweetener and some creamer. "But you seemed very deep in thought just now for such a young lady. May I ask if everything is all right?"

Kate's bang had fallen in her eye, and she brushed it back, tucking it behind her ear. She sighed. "Well, I just have a lot on my mind right now."

"Please"—he motioned for her to sit across from him—"let's talk about it."

She looked around. There were only two other customers in the restaurant, and they were already being taken care of by other members of the wait staff. So she sat down.

"I'm Ray, by the way." He stretched out his hand.

She shook it. "I'm Kate."

"It's nice to meet you, Kate. And forgive me if this is out of line, but I couldn't help but notice you seem to be expecting."

Kate looked down and rubbed her belly. "Yeah. It's getting tough to hide it at this point."

"I can see why you have a lot on your mind then." He listened quietly, giving her the opportunity to open up.

Kate hesitated for a moment. Then she said, "You teach others about religion, right?"

"Yes," he said proudly.

"Well, what religion do *you* practice?"

He sipped his coffee casually. "You'd be amazed how seldom I get asked that question. But to answer honestly, I don't follow any religion."

"Really? Why is that?"

"Well, anything that can be studied is subject to human error. Religion is a man-made entity, so it's hard to convince me that any one religion has it right."

The corner of Kate's mouth crinkled. "Makes sense."

"But that's not what you *really* want to ask, is it?"

"I guess not," she admitted.

"You really want to know if I believe in God, don't you?"

Slowly, she nodded.

"Do *you*, Kate?"

She looked out the window and then back at Ray. "I don't know... I mean, I think there was a time when I did...when I was really young...before I grew up. Then I really started to question everything."

"Like what?"

She sighed deeply. "My parents died when I was too young to remember them. I sometimes think, if there *is* a God, why would he take *both* of them from me? Why wouldn't he leave *somebody*, some relative or friend, to take care of me? Why was I thrown into the system only to get hurt and tossed around over and over?" She patted her stomach. "And why would I get pregnant when I'm so not ready to be a mom?"

"You've been through a lot for being so young."

"I'm twenty-seven. Sometimes I feel like I'm thirty-seven, and then other times I feel like I'm still fifteen."

"So by your logic, the existence of a God would mean that only good things would happen to you?"

"Well, no. It just seems like so many other people have it so good and others have it so bad. If God is real, does he pick and choose who gets all the good luck and who gets all the bad luck?"

He shook his head. "I don't think it works that way. All people suffer and go through hardships. It's just that some of us are better at hiding it than others. Trust me. Eavesdrop on your customers' conversations sometime. You'll be surprised by how many problems people have."

"So do *you* believe in God?"

"Absolutely," he answered without hesitation.

"Why?"

"Same reason I don't practice one religion—I've researched."

Kate had a perplexed look on her face. "But in all of that research, is there any piece of evidence that proves God truly exists?"

"Nope. That's why they call it *faith*."

"I don't get it." Kate shrugged.

"The point is not to find proof, Kate. The point is that so many people in so many different parts of the world at different times and in different ways all did the same thing. They determined that something or someone greater than ourselves is out there and has a hand in everything. You can call it fate, serendipity, God, or whatever, but I have no doubt that it exists."

"So why would God allow good things to happen to bad people and bad things to happen to good people?"

He scratched his head. "I also believe in relativity. Most people are not all good or all bad. We're human. We're flawed. I think when good things happen, those are *blessings,* and when bad things happen, those are *challenges.* We can be thankful for the good stuff and we can expect to grow from the bad stuff. I mean, is there any other healthy way to look at it?'

Suddenly, a group of customers came in the door.

"I'm next on the seating rotation," Kate said. "I'd better get back to work." She rose slowly, trying not to hit her belly on the booth as she stood. "Thanks for the talk."

"You're welcome." Ray smiled.

"By the way, are you also a therapist?"

He chuckled. "I hear that a lot, but no, I'm not. Let's just say, therapy is sort of a part of my life."

Chapter 33

Tuesday evening at the diner after ACDP meetings had become a weekly tradition for Daphne and Rachel. One evening in April, the two of them sat across from each other bantering and giggling. There was a brief break in the conversation when the waiter brought them their order—two grilled chicken salads with vinaigrette dressing and a basket of whole grain rolls to share.

"Thank you," Rachel said to the waiter, unrolling her napkin and taking out her silverware.

"Yes, thank you," said Daphne. "This looks *great*."

"You're welcome," the waiter said politely. He disappeared into the kitchen.

"By the way," Daphne said, "I meant to tell you, you look like you've lost weight."

"Oh, thanks," Rachel said shyly. "Not much. Only about five pounds."

"Still," said Daphne, "it looks like the family walks are paying off."

"Having dinner with you helps too."

"Really?" she asked just before taking her first bite. "How's that?"

"Let's just say you inspire me."

Daphne finished chewing and swallowing the mouthful of food. "Hmm, I don't think I've ever *inspired* anyone before."

Rachel finished her own bite. "How's Renee doing?"

"Good," said Daphne, reaching for a roll and tearing off a piece. "Her hair has grown back, and she's wearing it in a pixie cut. It looks adorable."

"Oh, that's great!"

"Yeah, it's hard to believe that six months ago, she was barely able to get out of bed. Now I can't get her on the phone anymore because she's out rollerblading or gardening or out to the movies."

"I'm so happy she's better, Daphne."

Daphne sighed deeply. "Me too."

They ate in silence for a minute or two.

"So," Rachel said, "not to bring up a sore subject, but has there been any response to the video you posted back in January?"

Daphne stopped eating and picked at her salad with her fork. "No, not yet."

Rachel instantly regretted asking the question. "Well, don't feel bad. It still might happen. In the meantime, at least, you've got Renee. She obviously did a wonderful job raising you. And if it makes you feel any better, my mom and I don't even speak."

"How come?"

"She…wasn't as vigilant as I think people ought to be with their kids, and if she had been, maybe it would have kept me from going through certain things."

Daphne almost asked, but she didn't want to pry. "I'm sorry."

Rachel shrugged. "Weird, isn't it? You're trying to find your biological mom, while I know exactly who mine is and I don't want to talk to her. You must think I'm stupid."

"It's not stupid. It's how you feel. And I'm certainly not one to judge. I'm far from perfect."

"Are you *kidding*? You're like exactly the kind of person I wish I could be. You're strong, beautiful, independent…"

Daphne couldn't stand receiving any more accolades that she didn't deserve. "I'm also a liar," she interrupted.

The corners of Rachel's mouth dropped.

"I go to ACDP meetings…and…I don't *have* a parent who is deceased."

"What?" Rachel leaned back in her seat.

"I don't have a dead parent. Well, not to my knowledge, I mean. So there. You see? I'm a fraud."

Rachel looked away for a minute and sighed loudly. "So why did you start going?"

"The truth is, for a while there, I really thought I was going to lose Renee. And I guess I figured being around people who've lost a parent might help me sort of prepare for what was coming."

Rachel felt the tightness in her chest begin to loosen. "Well," she said softly, "maybe there are some things in life you can't prepare for."

Daphne nodded sadly. "I'm so embarrassed."

"Why?"

"Because here I am sitting in front of *you*, who *has* suffered a loss. It makes my issues seem so insignificant. I was so impressed when you stood up and shared the story about your dad at the meeting. That took so much courage."

Rachel had let go of her fork. Under the table, she began scratching the backs of her hands and her wrists.

"And the *way* you told the story, it was so detailed. It was almost like we cou—"

Rachel stared blankly at her.

Daphne's eyes widened. "Oh my gosh, Rachel, how *did* you know what happened to your dad with so much detail?"

Rachel swallowed and licked her bottom lip. Then she whispered, "Because I was there."

Chapter 34

A few days later the diner had just opened for breakfast. With the exception of the kitchen staff, Kate and Pete were the only people there. They were rolling up silverware into paper napkins and lining them up while they talked.

"A baby shower?" Kate asked in dismay. "I don't know, Pete."

"Please, Kate," implored Pete. "It would mean so much to Elizabeth."

Ugh, he knows my weakness. "I wouldn't even know who to invite. I don't have any friends."

"Darling, I'm sure you have many friends."

"Well, I wouldn't feel comfortable anyway. A room full of people?... ME as the center of attention?...It's just not my thing."

"But you need things for the baby. Do you even have a bassinet?"

Kate shrugged. "There's still time. I'll figure it out. I promise I'll get whatever the baby needs before my due date."

Pete huffed loudly. He knew there was no convincing her. Plus, customers were starting to walk in the door. "Okay," he said softly, "but at least, let us buy a gift for the baby."

Good ole Pete. "Okay," she said with a smile. "Thank you."

He patted her on the back and started walking to the door to welcome the customers.

Chapter 35

Daphne was working at her desk, watching the clock. Currently, it showed eleven twenty-five a.m. *Five more minutes to lunch. Good! I'm starving.* It had been hard enough focusing on work that morning before the midmorning hunger came. Her mind kept wandering off to her last conversation with Rachel at dinner. *She was there when her father was killed. Gosh! I just can't imagine what she went through. I wish I could do something for her.*

Finally, at eleven thirty, she picked up her lunch sack and a bottle of water. She strutted to the break room, which her law firm shared with the insurance adjusters that worked on the same floor. As she approached the door, she noticed two women sitting together at one of the round tables. Both were in their forties and were dressed in simple clothes and comfortable shoes. They also appeared to be fighting "the battle of the bulge." One of them was sitting with her back to the door, while the other was facing it. They'd been conversing happily when the door squeaked open.

"Hello," Daphne said, stepping inside. She smiled at them.

They stopped talking. The lady with her back to the door turned around to see who had spoken. She looked at Daphne from head to toe, turned around again, and took another bite of her salad.

"Hi," the other woman said to Daphne with a disengenuine smile.

Okay, I guess I'll just warm up my lunch and leave then.

She walked over to the microwave. Her back was to the two women having lunch. She pulled her entrée out of its box and used a plastic fork from her lunch sack to stab holes in the plastic film. As she placed the fork down and pulled the microwave door open, she heard them whispering.

Don't worry. That probably has nothing to do with you.

She placed her lunch in the microwave and set it to cook for three minutes. *But why are they whispering? And why did they stop talking when I walked in the door?*

Then the giggling started.

Seriously? I just came in to heat up my food! What have I done to these women?!

Relax. Again, that may have nothing to do with you.

Well, I'm not so sure.

Even if it does, you can't change it. If they want to snub you, that's their problem. They don't even know you. Just go eat somewhere else.

The microwave finally dinged. Daphne pulled the door open, grabbed a paper towel from a nearby dispenser, and used it to protect her fingers from the heat as she pulled out her entrée. She carefully peeled back the plastic film and dropped it into the trash can that was sitting beside the counter. Then she grabbed an extra paper towel, folded it, and slid it underneath her tray. With her lunch in tow, she turned and began walking toward the door. "Have a nice day," she said as she used her back to open the door. She walked out and let the door swing shut behind her.

In the break room, Agnes and Betty began talking again.

"Have a nice day, you skinny bitch!" Agnes joked.

Betty busted out laughing.

"How many calories do you think are in her lunch?" Agnes asked rhetorically.

"Probably about three hundred at best," said Betty.

"It's not like it matters, though. I've seen her walking around the building during her breaks, so she's probably burning them off."

"Geez, obsess much?"

"Right?"

They both laughed.

Outside, Daphne found an empty picnic table and sat down to eat lunch by herself.

I'm tired of feeling like the new kid at school every day.

That's all right. We have our social media to keep us company.

Daphne took her cell phone out of her pocket. She opened up the app to check her account with one hand and took a bite of her organic, gluten-free enchilada with the other.

She scrolled through and read all of her notifications, reacting and commenting when appropriate. Next, she checked her e-mails. She began clearing the messages that were clearly junk mail, a handful at a time, until there was nothing left.

Still no response. A knot formed in the pit of Daphne's stomach. She could barely bring herself to finish the last few bites of food that were left. However, she forced herself to do so and then took a few sips of her water. When she was done, she sat in silence. She looked around. The grass was neatly cut, and the trees and bushes were perfectly pruned. It reminded Daphne of a cemetery—without the headstones.

The day was sunny and warm but not too hot or humid for springtime. With no one to talk to and nothing else to do, Daphne decided to take a walk around the grounds for the last ten minutes of her lunch break.

Chapter 36

"Rachel," Dr. Nova said, sitting down across from her in her office. "I'm so glad you came back. It's been so long I was worried I scared you off the last time, especially since you canceled the next session."

"Yeah, I'm sorry about that," said Rachel, "I've been feeling a little better, actually, so I sort of put it on hold. I've been spending time with a new friend and exercising more."

"Yeah, good job, by the way. Looks like you're getting in good physical shape."

"Thanks. I'm definitely feeling better…stronger."

"That's great, Rachel. You should be proud of yourself."

Rachel shrugged.

"But you obviously felt the need to come in today."

Rachel nodded. "I just don't want to fall into the same trap as before, feeling like everything is fine for weeks or even months at a time. And then suddenly—*Bam!* Something triggers me, and then I'm right back to where I was."

"Well, it's very encouraging that you realized that on your own."

"The last time I was here, it seemed like we were on the brink of a watershed moment. I think I'm ready."

Dr. Nova took a deep breath. "Then let's begin."

Rachel sat up straight in her chair. *Don't be afraid.*

"So," the doctor began, "we're going to do some visualization to help you with this."

"Okay," she said apprehensively.

"You're going to close your eyes and picture Baylee when she was little. And you're going to say the things that you wish you could say to her."

A lump formed in Rachel's throat.

"This is going to feel awkward. And it may take you doing this multiple times to get it right. But I promise it will help."

Rachel inhaled and exhaled deeply.

"When you think of Baylee, what place comes to mind? What surroundings?"

"That's easy. The backyard, under the deck, where she used to hide from her dad."

"Perfect. Close your eyes."

Rachel complied and continued to listen to the sound of Dr. Nova's voice.

"I want you to breathe in through your nose slowly, filling your lungs with air completely, and hold it for three seconds. Then exhale as slowly as you can…and then do that three times."

When Rachel had finished, Dr. Nova proceeded.

"Imagine yourself walking out of that house, as you are today. What do you see around you? Under you? Above you?"

"The sky is overcast. The grass is dry and lifeless. There's trees in the distance."

"Okay, good. Do you see the deck?"

Rachel, with her eyes still closed, turned her head. "Yes."

"I want you to walk toward it and look for Baylee."

In her vision, Rachel saw herself walking closer and closer to the edge of the deck. She could hear her sneakers, crunching on the grass with each step. Then she stood in front of the deck and looked down. She took a deep breath and slowly got on her hands and knees. She looked underneath and saw Baylee sitting with her knees to her chest.

"I see her," Rachel said to Dr. Nova.

"Okay, good. I want you to talk to her."

"What do I say?"

"You'll figure it out. Just trust yourself."

Rachel focused on her vision again. She crawled toward Baylee and sat in front of her. "Hi, Baylee," she said gently.

"Hi," said Baylee without making eye contact.

"Can I talk to you?"

Baylee nodded.

"I...know what your dad has done."

Baylee looked at Rachel with wide eyes. "I'm not supposed to talk about that."

"I know, and it's okay. You don't have to say anything."

Baylee rested her head on her knees.

"But I want to tell you something."

She looked up again.

"What your dad is doing is not your fault. I know you might feel like there's something wrong with you, but there's not. There's something wrong with *him*."

"Rachel," Dr. Nova said, "our time is almost up."

In her vision, Rachel said, "I need to go, Baylee."

Baylee suddenly let go of her knees and sat up on them. "Please don't go!"

Rachel felt herself start to cry. "I have to, Baylee. I'm sorry."

"No!" cried Baylee.

Rachel wanted to throw up as she forced herself to swivel her body around and crawl out from under the deck. Her tears came harder and splashed as they landed in the dirt.

"Don't go!" Baylee kept calling.

"Rachel, I'm going to count down from five," Dr. Nova said. "And when I get to one, you're going to open your eyes. Ready? Five..."

Rachel reached the edge of the deck and continued to cry. She could still hear Baylee screaming, "Don't go!"

"Four..."

She looked up at the sky, trying to tune out the sound of Baylee's voice.

"Three..."

Rachel breathed in slowly, filling her lungs with air.

"Two..."

She began to exhale.

"One."

Rachel opened her eyes and looked at Dr. Nova, shaking.

"Are you okay?"

Rachel's crying intensified. "I can't let her go!" she yelled. "She's just a little girl! She has *nobody*! I can't let her go!"

Chapter 37

Kate waited in Dr. Wyatt's office, on the examining table. Being in her third trimester, the awkward paper gowns were now a thing of the past. During the last few visits, all she'd had to do was pull her shirt up, and the doctor used the sticky glob on her belly and a transducer to see the baby. This visit, however, was different from the previous ones. This time, she wasn't alone.

"How are you feeling?" asked Adam, who had been sitting in a nearby chair.

"Good," Kate answered without expression.

Adam looked unconvinced.

"I don't know." She shook her head. "I just have this weird feeling, like something's wrong."

"With the baby?" Adam stood up and walked over to her. He rubbed her back gently.

Kate sighed. "Not sure." Suddenly, they heard a knock, and Dr. Wyatt stuck her head in through the doorway. "Hi, Kate," she said cheerfully. She walked in and closed the door behind her.

"Hi, Dr. Wyatt," said Kate.

"And is this the baby's father?" she asked, looking at Adam.

Before Adam could say anything, Kate interjected, "Yes. This is Adam." She smiled.

Adam smiled back at Kate like a shy puppy. Then he shook Dr. Wyatt's hand. "It's nice to meet you."

"Likewise," Dr. Wyatt smiled. "So we're getting close, huh? Are you guys ready?"

Kate shook her head slowly.

Dr. Wyatt chuckled. "I remember that feeling with my first!" She patted Kate on the shoulder.

"Dr. Wyatt?" Adam said. "Before you came in, Kate was saying that she had a weird feeling, like something might be wrong."

She turned to Kate and leaned in to look her in the eyes. "Hey, everything will be fine. Everything up until now has been perfect. It's probably just first-time-mom jitters."

"I hope so," Kate said.

"Well, let me see if I can put your minds at ease." She looked at Adam and then back at Kate. "You know the drill," she told her.

Kate laid back and lifted her shirt. Dr. Wyatt squirted the cold goop onto Kate's stomach, making her belly twitch slightly. Adam's eyes, seeing her stomach up close for the first time since Kate became pregnant, widened with amazement. Next, the doctor took out the transducer and began to rub it around Kate's stomach. She turned on the machine.

For a moment, all was silent as Dr. Wyatt listened for the sound of the baby's heartbeat. Suddenly, it broke through, startling Adam.

"Sorry," said Dr. Wyatt. "I'll turn the volume down."

Ba-boom. Ba-boom. Ba-boom.

"Holy cow!" Adam laughed.

Kate giggled. "I know. It's pretty crazy, right?"

Dr. Wyatt continued to move the transducer around until they got a clear image of the baby on the screen. "And there you go," she sang happily, pointing to the screen.

Adam's jaw dropped. It was a perfectly formed baby. He could see everything—a little profile of its face, a chubby belly, ten fingers, ten toes, and its little heart flickering a mile a minute. He sighed deeply but didn't say a word.

"The baby looks absolutely perfect," the doctor assured them. "The head is the right size, the heart and lungs are developing normally. There's no sign of trouble, Kate. You can rest easy."

"That's great," Adam said in relief. "Thank you so much."

Dr. Wyatt turned to Kate. "Now I know you said you didn't want to know the gender, but have you reconsidered?"

Kate turned to Adam "I guess if you want to know, we can go ahead and find out."

Adam nodded enthusiastically. "Yes, please."

Kate looked at Dr. Wyatt. "Okay."

The doctor wiggled in her swivel stool and changed the angle of the transducer on Kate's belly so that they could see between the baby's legs. "You're having a girl!"

Adam's heart skipped a beat. His nose stung and he could feel the urge to cry, but he stopped himself. "That's awesome!" he said in a voice as tough as he could muster.

Kate only smiled. *I knew it.*

After the appointment, Adam drove Kate home. He pulled his blue two-door sedan onto the street in front of her house and left the engine running.

As soon as the car stopped, the baby began to move. "You want to see something cool?" Kate asked.

"Uh, sure," Adam answered, confused. He had expected her to just go inside.

"Promise you won't think it's weird?"

He laughed. "I promise I'll *try* not to think that."

Kate reclined her seat all the way back. She pulled her shirt up and waited. Within seconds, she felt the baby's movement again. This time, it was so intense that it made her stomach move. It looked like the baby was trying to push her way out and then rolled to another spot and tried to push through again.

"Oh my gosh!" Adam exclaimed. "Does that hurt?"

Kate laughed. "No. It just feels funny."

The baby continued to do the same thing for a few minutes. Kate and Adam looked on in wonder until she settled down again.

Adam sighed. "Well, thank you for showing me that...and for letting me come today."

"Thank you for taking me," she said. "I should've asked you sooner. You have a right to be there."

"Well, you asked me now. That's what matters."

Kate frowned.

"What's wrong?"

"I know Dr. Wyatt said everything is fine," she said sadly, "but…"

"You're still worried." He finished her sentence.

"It's just a feeling I can't shake," she said. Then she looked him in the eye imploringly. "I'm scared, Adam."

He grabbed her hand and held it. "You heard what she said about first-time jitters. I'm sure it's scary as hell going through what you're going through. But you're not alone, Kate. I'll be there for you as much as you want me to be."

She took a deep breath. "Well, now that we know it's a girl, maybe we could go pick some stuff out for her this weekend."

"Sure," he said.

With that, Kate opened the door and placed one foot on the pavement. "I'll text you. We can figure out when."

"Okay." He made sure she was inside the house before driving away.

Kate walked in and was immediately startled by a large object that was sitting on the couch. *What is that?* She walked into the living room to investigate. It was an oversized, plush teddy bear. The coffee table was covered with wrapped gift boxes and bags of various sizes. But it didn't stop there. Leaning against the wall that led to her bedroom were several economy size boxes of diapers and wipes. She couldn't believe her eyes.

"Who did this?" she said out loud. She looked all around the kitchen and living room for clues, but there was no card or note. She walked over to the bedroom and was surprised once again. Beside her bed was a small bassinet with a button that made it rock. Inside the bassinet, there was a baby's receiving blanket and a yellow envelope. Kate picked up the envelope and carefully opened it. She took out the card, which had images of rattles, footie pajamas, and diaper pins on the cover. When she opened it, she saw that it had been signed by everyone who worked at the diner. Instantly, she became so overwhelmed with joy and gratitude that she began to cry.

Maybe Pete and Adam are right. Maybe I do have friends. Maybe I'm not alone.

She held the card to her heart and wiped a tear away. It was then that she looked down and realized that she was still wearing her shoes. She'd forgotten to take them off before she crossed from the foyer to the living room. And to her surprise, she didn't care.

Chapter 38

Daphne was sitting by herself in her apartment. She was curled up on the couch in an old T-shirt and shorts, scrolling through the channels on her TV but nothing appealed to her. She needed a distraction to keep her from obsessing over the lack of response to her video.

Conrad. She got up and grabbed her cell phone off the dining room table and scrolled through her contacts until she found his name. It rang only twice.

"Hello, beautiful," he answered.

"Hi," she said flirtatiously. "How are you?"

"Good, thanks. How are *you?*"

Terrible. She sighed. "No complaints."

"It's funny, I was going to call you anyway. I have a bit of news."

"Oh?" she asked, intrigued.

"Yes. I've received a new job opportunity, and so it looks like I'll be relocating at the beginning of summer."

Daphne's mouth went dry. She could feel her heart start to flutter nervously. "Really?" she said casually. "Where would you be moving?"

"Ah, back to the UK, actually."

Her chest felt like it had just caved in. She swallowed. The tears were already coming. She sat completely still and let them roll down her cheeks and breathed as quietly as she could.

"Daph, are you there?"

"Uh-huh." She grabbed the bottom of her shirt and dried her eyes. She rubbed her nose quietly, being careful not to sniff. "That's definitely a big deal. Congratulations."

"Thank you, Daphne." He was quiet for a moment. Then he said, "I wasn't kidding when I said I fancy you."

Daphne nodded. She began crying harder but still did not make a sound. Finally, she spoke. "I believe you. It's just…bad timing, I guess."

"Well, do you think I could see you again before I leave? I might need a farewell shag."

She giggled.

He waited for her to answer.

"Um, I'm not sure that's a good idea, Conrad. It's probably better that we just remember it the way it was. You know, without drama. No long-winded goodbyes, that sort of thing."

He sighed. "Well, it was worth a shot. But I do understand."

"Thank you, Conrad."

"For what, Daph?"

"Just…thank you…for everything."

"Well, then…" He paused. "Cheers, Daphne."

"Cheers," she said bravely and hung up. She held the phone against her forehead for a moment. The tears wouldn't stop. Suddenly, she chugged the phone at the wall. Upon impact, a small piece of the cell phone case chipped off and landed on the carpet. The phone itself landed in a different spot. Her hands shook. She hugged herself tightly. *Not again, damn it! This wasn't supposed to hurt!*

Chapter 39

It was late in the afternoon the following Monday. Rachel and Lee were on their walk with the kids. Lee was pushing Nick in his stroller. Avery was riding her tricycle a few yards ahead of them.

"Maybe I should cancel my appointment for tomorrow," Rachel said.

"Why?" asked Lee.

"Because it got a little uncomfortable the last time."

"I don't think it's supposed to be comfortable. I think that's the point. If you're going to grow, it might feel awkward in the beginning."

Rachel huffed, in part from the cardio work. "It was embarrassing too. We did this visualization exercise, and then afterward I couldn't stop crying."

"Do you think you're the first patient to cry like that in front of Dr. Nova?"

"Probably not," Rachel admitted.

"Babe, you can do whatever you want to do. I just think you'll feel better if you finish what you've started."

"I guess."

"You should go. Besides, it'll probably be easier the second time now that the first one is out of the way. And don't forget, you still went to your meeting and out to dinner with Daphne after the first one, right?"

"True," she said. "I guess with all of that crying out of my system, it was actually easier to maintain composure around people after that."

"See? It's working already and you don't even realize it. Six months ago, you would've come home after that session and hidden from the world."

Rachel nodded. "I would have, wouldn't I?" She cracked a smile.

Lee stopped for a moment, placed his arm around her shoulder, and kissed her forehead. "I'm proud of you."

She huffed again. "Okay. You're right. I'll go tomorrow."

* * *

At the diner, Kate had just written down an order for a couple that was sitting at one of the booths. She thanked them both and smiled. She continued smiling as she walked over to where everyone taped up the tickets. "Here's another order for you, Blake," she said to the line cook standing closest to her.

"Thanks, Kate," he answered with a wink.

"You're welcome," she said, making eye contact.

Between serving customers, Kate performed her usual cleaning rituals. But it was different now. It felt different. Being just weeks away from giving birth, one would think she would have been dragging around slowly and acting cranky. But instead, there was a spring in her step that she'd never had before. *What is wrong with you? You're so...happy?*

Was it the unexpected kindness that her coworkers had bestowed upon her? Or was it Adam? She couldn't decide.

As she was wiping down one of the tables, Kate suddenly felt a sharp pain that immobilized her. *Oh! What is that?*

"Are you okay?" another waitress named Bonnie asked. She had seen what happened and walked over to Kate. She placed her hand on her back.

Kate put her hands on the table she'd been cleaning and leaned on it. Her eyes were shut tightly. She took a deep breath and exhaled slowly until the pain subsided. "Yeah," she said, slowly opening her eyes and rubbing her lower abdomen. "This pain just came from out of nowhere. I've never felt anything like that before. It just sort of caught me off guard."

"You're almost due, right?" asked Bonnie.

"Three more weeks," Kate answered.

"Well, take it easy," she patted her on the back and walked away.

"Thanks," Kate said. She waited a moment before resuming work. Her smile was less bright after that.

Chapter 40

Daphne had taken a personal day. Between the perceived rejection from her birth mother (yet again), Conrad's announcement, and the stress at work, she needed a break. She had tossed and turned all through the night and was still groggy when the sun came up. She laid in bed for a while, staring at the ceiling.

When she couldn't stand lying there any longer, she kicked the covers off and rolled out of bed, leaving it unmade. She pulled off her T-shirt and pajama shorts and threw them haphazardly into the hamper. Then she put on her workout clothes and sneakers, brushed her teeth, and went to the kitchen. She grabbed a bottle of water from the refrigerator and her earbuds off the dining room table. Suddenly, she remembered that she'd left her cell phone on the bedroom nightstand.

Ugh! She stumbled back to get it. When she grabbed the phone and looked at it, she saw that she had a missed call. For a moment, her heart leapt. But it was from an unknown number, and the caller did not leave a message. *Don't be a fool, Daphne. He's not going to call. It's over.*

Once she was at the gym, Daphne wasted little time preparing to work off her aggression. She did a quick three-minute stretch and then hopped onto the elliptical machine. She plugged her earbuds into her phone and cranked up the music. She hit Start on the machine and began pedaling slowly. Her muscles were already tired and tense from lack of sleep. She pushed through it.

As she pedaled in time with the music, her mind drifted. She imagined her birth mother swaddling her as a newborn and placing her inside that tiny cardboard box. She wondered, *Did she hold me for any length of time? Or did she just leave? Did she cry when she left me? Did she feel anything?* Daphne pedaled harder and turned the music up.

She thought about Brock. She envisioned what he had looked like on the day he left, when she was twelve. He tried so hard to explain why he was leaving and swore it had nothing to do with her. When they hugged goodbye, she had wanted to latch on harder— hard enough that he couldn't leave.

Daphne increased the intensity level on the machine and pushed harder.

She pictured Conrad the last time she saw him, looking as handsome as ever. The way they made each other laugh. The warmth of his body against hers. The gentle way he held her.

Daphne knew she would never feel that again.

She turned the music up even louder and pedaled as hard as she could, faster and faster. Her legs burned. Her heart felt like it was about to beat out of her chest. Her lungs began to tighten, making it harder to catch her breath. The pain intensified, but she kept pushing, harder and harder until she couldn't bear it anymore.

She slowed her pace. She breathed in as deeply as she could and then exhaled loudly. She kept pedaling at a snail's pace, not wanting to stop. *Come on, Daphne! You can take it! Push through!*

But she couldn't.

Accepting defeat, she stopped completely. *Damn it!* She turned off the machine, laid her head on the console, and cried.

Chapter 41

Not only did Rachel keep her appointment with Dr. Nova. She moved it to the morning when the doctor had an opening. Anytime she felt herself starting to lose her nerve, she remembered her conversation with Lee. *He thinks I can do it. Maybe I should think that too.*

She took a deep breath before exiting the car. She sauntered up to the door with as much confidence as she could summon and rang the bell.

Dr. Nova opened the door. "Hey, Rachel," she said, holding it open for her. "Glad you made it."

"Thanks," Rachel said. "How are you?"

"Oh, I'm fine," said Dr. Nova. "Let's talk about you." She motioned for Rachel to go into her office. Once they were inside, the doctor shut the door. "I know the last time was a little heavy. I was wondering how you're doing with that."

They both sat down.

Rachel sighed. "Well, it was rough, obviously."

Dr. Nova nodded. "It was."

"And whenever I think about it, I feel a little embarrassed."

"Why would you be embarrassed?"

"Because…I couldn't control my emotions. They just poured out like a waterfall, and I felt like I couldn't stop it."

"May I ask you something specific about that moment…when your emotions felt like they were too much?"

"Sure."

"Your exact words at the time were 'I can't let her go. She's just a little girl. She has nobody.' Is it possible…that you weren't talking about Baylee?"

Rachel furrowed her brow.

"There was another time that you felt alone like that, too, wasn't there? You were hiding, too, and needed someone to come pull you out."

Rachel looked like a deer in headlights. She began scratching her hands and wrists but quickly stopped as soon as she realized what she was doing. "I haven't thought about that in a really long time."

"I know," Dr. Nova said gently. "But I would encourage you to think about it now so you can see the connection."

Rachel closed her eyes. She took a deep breath in slowly and let it out. As she recalled the horrific event, she described it to Dr. Nova. "My father," she sighed, "was closing up shop. I had toys that I played with in the back room, and he told me to go in there and put them away…" She paused.

"It's okay, Rachel. You're completely safe."

Rachel began to cry. "That's when he came in…and he had a gun…I didn't know he had a gun until he fired it. He said 'Give me the money in the safe.' As soon as I heard that, I ran and hid under a table."

"You must have been terrified."

She cried more. "I was…I heard my dad say 'There is no safe. Just take the jewelry and go.' They went back and forth for a minute. There was a pause…then I heard the gunfire."

Dr. Nova sighed deeply, trying not to cry herself.

"I heard glass shattering. He was getting as much jewelry as he could before running off."

"And you were under that table all alone, weren't you?"

Rachel nodded. "I just froze under there. I couldn't move. I just waited."

"Who were you waiting for?"

Her voice became weak. "My mom. I just wanted my mom."

"Who found you under that table, Rachel?"

She wiped her tears and grabbed a tissue from the end table beside her. "A police officer." She blew her nose.

"So a stranger came for you, not your mom."

"Yeah." She nodded continuously.

"Tell me how that made you feel."

"Disappointed…lonely. Like I couldn't count on her."

"When you look back on it now as an adult, what do you really think happened? Do you think that your mom didn't want to find you?"

"I never thought about it," Rachel said. She took a deep breath. "Maybe they wouldn't let her in because it was the scene of a crime?"

"Where was she?" Dr. Nova asked.

Rachel tried to recall that night in more detail. She remembered the moment when the police officer found her. At first, she'd been afraid to take his hand when he held it out to her. But after he told her that her mother was waiting outside, she took his hand and pulled herself out from under the table. The officer held her hand the entire time he escorted her to the door. As soon as they emerged, Deborah jumped forward, scooped Rachel up, and hugged her. "She was just outside," Rachel answered. "The whole time."

"Do you believe she wanted to be in there, looking for you?"

Rachel remembered how tightly Deborah had held her, like a baby, like she didn't want to let go. "I want to believe that."

"Believe it," Dr. Nova said passionately. Her eyes were suddenly glassy from tears forming. "There's not a doubt in my mind that your mother would've pulled you out of there if she could have."

"And the time after that?"

"Again, I truly believe she would've pulled you out of *that* if she could have…if she had known what was going on."

"I just don't understand how she couldn't have known!"

"You'll have to ask her about that, Rachel," she said. "I know you don't want to, but I don't think you'll be able to heal if you don't. It's like a swamp—you can't go around it, you can't go over it, you can't go under it. You have to go through it."

Rachel sighed loudly.

"You're still hiding under that table, Rachel. And you can't shake the image of Baylee hiding under that deck because you know that feeling all too well. People violated you, not once but twice."

Rachel cringed.

"I don't blame you for being closed off, but at some point, you have to let yourself say 'It's okay' and start moving on."

Rachel looked out the window for a moment and then at Dr. Nova. "Sometimes I wonder if there's such a thing as 'normal' anymore."

"What do you mean by 'normal'?"

"You know, a 'normal,' happy childhood. Parents who stay together and die at a ripe, old age. No dysfunction. No drama. Does that even exist anymore?"

Dr. Nova shook her head. "I hate to break it to you, Rachel, but what you're describing is almost nonexistent these days. There's a new 'normal' now. There's so much dysfunction in the world it touches nearly everyone."

Rachel began to look depressed.

"But do you want to hear the good news?" The doctor smiled.

Rachel nodded.

"It means you're not alone...far from it."

Chapter 42

It was almost lunchtime, and Adam was sitting at his cubicle in a polo shirt and khakis, typing away at his computer. He heard his phone vibrate and stopped working. When he realized it was Kate, he immediately checked the message: "I think I'm having contractions."

Adam quickly got to his feet. "Dean," he said to his coworker in the next cubicle, "I've got to step out. It's Kate."

"No problem, buddy." Dean waved at him.

Adam power walked all the way to a door marked "Stairs." He pushed the door open and jogged all the way down the steps. When he got to the first floor, he threw open a second door and stepped outside. The bright light of the sun surprised him at first, but his eyes quickly adjusted. He hit the voice command button on his phone and spoke into it. "Call Kate." There was a pause followed by a dial tone.

Kate answered on the third ring. "Hey," she said quietly.

"Hey. Are you okay? Where are you?"

She sighed. "I'm at home. Just lying on the couch. I'm okay so far."

"Are you sure it's labor?"

"Well, I sort of had a pain like this before, and I thought it was the same thing this time. But I've had a bunch of them since six o'clock this morning."

Adam swallowed nervously. "I mean, it's almost your exact due date, right? That means this could be it."

Kate shrugged on the other end. "Your guess is as good as mine."

"I'm coming over," he said boldly.

Kate sighed. "Okay."

They hung up.

Fifteen minutes later, Adam knocked on the door. He waited patiently, figuring she'd probably need a moment to come to the door. But when she didn't answer, he tried the doorknob. It turned and he went inside. "Kate?" he called.

Kate was still lying on the couch. She raised her arm, signaling him to come closer.

He quickly slipped off his loafers and walked over to her. She was laid out on the sofa, beads of perspiration on her forehead. She was breathing heavily. "What's wrong?" he asked.

Kate took one more deep breath and let it out loudly. "That was one of them...when you started knocking. Sorry I couldn't get up."

Adam tried not to laugh but couldn't help himself. "Sorry, I guess my timing sucks."

She looked at him with a tender smile. "Your timing is fine."

He knelt down beside her. "So do you think you're ready to go to the hospital?"

"Not yet," she answered. Then she began to sit up.

"Here," Adam said, standing. "Let me help you."

"I'm good," she said, sitting up now and leaning against one of the couch pillows. "Can we just sit here for a bit?"

"Yeah, of course." He sat down beside her on the couch.

Kate sighed deeply. She looked weak.

"Do you want me to get you anything?"

She shook her head slowly. "Thanks, anyway. I know you're trying to help."

Adam nodded. "I just don't really know what to do right now. I'm kind of freaking out."

Kate chuckled softly, rubbing her belly. "Isn't it funny? Not long ago, I was the one freaking out and you were the calm one. Now it's the opposite."

He smiled.

"Adam," she said, looking serious all of a sudden, "there's something I want to tell you."

His smile faded.

"I don't know if this is going to make sense, so I just need you to hear me and try to understand, okay?"

"All right."

"Remember when I said I'm not sure I'm 'mother material'?"

He nodded.

"Well, I guess maybe I'm not sure I'm 'falling in love' material either."

Adam's eyes dropped.

"But if I were, I think you're the one I'd fall in love with."

He looked up again. His heart was pounding. He didn't say a word.

Not long after that, Kate's water broke, and they left for the hospital.

Chapter 43

After her feeble attempt at a workout, Daphne decided to take herself out for coffee. She was waiting at a stoplight and checking her reflection in the mirror to make sure she looked "decent." Suddenly, her cell phone began ringing via Bluetooth. She looked down and read the name—Julie Costas. Daphne instantly recognized the name as Renee's neighbor. She furrowed her brow. *Why would Julie be calling?*

The driver behind her blasted his car horn impatiently, making her jump. She looked up and realized that the light had turned green. She waved apologetically at the driver in the rearview mirror. The phone continued to ring as she began to accelerate. On the fourth ring, she tapped the Answer button. Her heart was racing from having been startled. "Hello," she said, huffing for breath.

"Daphne?" Julie said.

"Yes, hi, Julie. Is everything okay?"

There was a pause before Julie spoke again. "Daphne, I'm at the hospital."

Daphne's heart sank. "W-What's going on? Is it Renee?" Quickly, she looked around for a place to park. There was a nearly vacant office lot at the next turn. She pulled in and slipped into one of the spaces.

"Yes…"

She put the car in park, took the phone off Bluetooth, and put it up to her ear. "What happened?"

Julie sighed. "Well, she's alive, first of all."

"Okay, good." Her heart was pounding harder now. "Do I need to come to the hospital?"

"I would," said Julie. "Daphne, she's in a coma."

Chapter 44

Rachel decided to take advantage of the time she had between her session with Dr. Nova and the ACDP meeting and do some grocery shopping. On her way home from the store, a message came from Daphne. Since she was driving, she used her car's Text Read-Aloud feature. With the tap of a few buttons, a robotic voice said Daphne's words: "Hey, Rachel. I won't be able to make it to the meeting today. I'm sorry. I'll explain later."

"Oh, that sucks," Rachel said to herself, pouting. As she slowed down to turn into her driveway, her heart sank. Deborah's car was parked in front of the house.

Shit!

Rachel parked her car and sat for a moment. Deborah got out of her vehicle, shut the door, and leaned against it. They stared at each other for a moment.

No time like the present. Go through the swamp, Rachel. She sighed deeply and turned off the car. Slowly, she opened the car door and stepped out.

Deborah took a step toward her. "Need help with those groceries?"

"Sure," Rachel answered calmly. She shut the door, turned around, and popped the trunk with the remote. They both walked somberly to the back of the car and started unloading bags of groceries. Then they walked to the door where Deborah waited for Rachel to unlock it. The silence continued until they entered the foyer.

"Would you mind leaving your shoes here?" Rachel requested.

"Not at all," Deborah answered.

They both removed their shoes and entered the kitchen.

"How about I take stuff out of bags and you put it away?" Deborah suggested. "I don't know where anything goes."

"Sounds good," Rachel answered, avoiding eye contact. "Thank you."

They were silent again. By the third empty grocery bag, Deborah couldn't take any more. "Rachel, I know something I did at some point caused you to shut me out. But you're my daughter, and I love you."

Rachel stopped putting groceries away and placed both hands on the counter. She locked her elbows and arched her back.

"Tell me what it is and I'll apologize."

She clenched her fists and squeezed her eyes tightly, fighting back the sobs. *Just say it, Rachel.* Her back remained turned. "You shouldn't have left me there."

"Where? At the Marshalls'? Are you still upset about that?"

She turned slowly. Her cheeks were flushed, and her breathing had quickened. "Don't I *look* upset?"

Deborah became impatient. "Stop! I am so over beating myself up for that! Rachel, your dad died. I had to go to work to support us. For God's sake, I'm not going to apologize for the fact that I had a *job!*"

Rachel became enraged. "Your *first* job was to be my *mother!* Your *job* was to *protect me* and *be there* for me!"

"I was! I did!"

"No, you didn't!"

"What are you talking about?"

"Where were you?" She yelled. "Where were you when that son of a bitch molested me when I was seven years old?"

"Who?"

"How can you not know? How could you not have known then?"

"Mr. Marshall?"

"Of course! Who else would it have been? And how could you not have known, Mom?"

Deborah threw her hand over her mouth, like she was going to throw up. After a moment, she removed it. "How was I supposed to know?"

"Damnit! Were you that blind? I started having night terrors! I was wetting the bed at night! How could you *not* know?"

"Honey, I thought—" She became choked up. She grabbed a kitchen chair and sat at the table, shaking. She looked out the window, unable to bear the pain in her daughter's eyes. "I thought you were having trouble dealing with your dad's murder."

"I was!" Rachel yelled. "This just made it worse!"

They both cried for a moment, each trying to pull herself together.

Deborah turned to look at Rachel again, who was leaning with her back against the kitchen sink, hugging herself. She shook like a frightened dog.

"Why didn't you tell me?" Deborah asked.

Rachel's crying turned to sobbing. This time, it was so hard that her mother almost couldn't understand her. "He told me that if I said anything to anyone, he was going to hurt Baylee and that no one would believe me, anyway." She covered her eyes and continued sobbing.

Deborah walked over to her and placed her hands on her shoulders. Rachel flinched

"Leave me alone, Mom! Damn it, you did it before!"

The words felt like a knife piercing Deborah in the heart. She sighed slowly. "Just let me ask you one more thing."

Rachel wiped her face and looked at her. She was beginning to calm down. "What?"

"Why didn't you tell me *after*? When you no longer went there anymore?"

She shook her head sadly. "What good would that have done? It was over then. I just wanted to pretend like it never happened."

Deborah breathed in and out slowly. "But you can't."

Again, she shook her head. "I tried and I tried. I keep trying all the time to be okay, but I'm *not* okay! My husband has to ask for *permission* to touch me, Mom. I dread the day that Avery asks to go to her first sleepover because I want to say no! I *am not* okay!"

"Rachel!" Deborah said sternly. "You didn't let me help you then, so let me help you now."

She huffed sarcastically, "How?"

"Sit down," she commanded, pointing to the kitchen table.

Rachel did as her mother said.

Deborah sat across from her and looked her square in the eye. "Rachel, the one who's not okay is *him*, not *you*. Anybody who takes advantage of children, especially a sweet, innocent little girl, is *sick* and *twisted*. You have *nothing* to be ashamed of. No reason to feel like it was your fault. And damn him *to hell* for what he did to you!"

Rachel's eyes were glued to her mother.

"Baby, I am *so sorry*. I'm sorry I didn't see the warning signs. I'm sorry I didn't hear you when you pleaded with me not to send you there… I'm sorry."

Rachel wanted to throw herself into her mother's arms and cry on her shoulder, but she couldn't move. She wanted to accept her apology, but she couldn't speak. She was completely frozen.

Suddenly, Deborah got up. She headed straight for the foyer and began putting her shoes on.

"Where are you going?" Rachel asked as she heard her open the front door.

The only response was the door slamming shut.

Chapter 45

Adam parked his car on the fourth-floor deck of the covered lot at the hospital. The first three levels had proven to be unlucky as he circled and scanned for an empty space on the way up. He set the vehicle to park and carefully helped Kate out of the passenger side. She leaned against the car while he retrieved her suitcase from the back seat. Then he threw it over his shoulder and put his arm around Kate. "Let's go."

Kate put her arm around his waist to keep her balance. She shuffled softly all the way to the entrance. Adam patiently kept her pace. This continued all the way to the maternity ward help desk. Once there, Kate reached for the counter with both hands for support, bracing herself for another contraction.

"Hi," Adam said to a woman at the help desk, "um, we're having a baby."

A curly-haired woman in fuchsia scrubs looked apologetically at Adam. "I'm so sorry, sir. You'll have to go to the first floor to check her in. This is where mothers come *after* they've had their babies."

"Seriously?" he complained.

Kate was taken aback. She'd never seen him mad before. "It's okay." She patted his arm. "Let's just go there." She turned clumsily and began looking for signs indicating where to go.

"The elevators are just behind you on the left-hand side." The nurse pointed.

Adam turned to her. "Thank you…and sorry."

"It's okay," she assured him. "Good luck."

175

Adam took hold of Kate again and helped her to the elevator. He pushed the button marked "1" and put the suitcase down for a moment. He rubbed Kate's back as she pressed her head against the wall and gripped the rails tightly. "How's it going?"

Kate gritted her teeth. "Contraction!" she huffed.

He continued to rub. "Okay, hang on. We're almost there."

The elevator chimed and came to a halt. Kate abruptly turned around, took a deep breath, and grabbed Adam's arm tightly. The doors opened, and they saw a woman who had obviously been waiting to go up. She was about to step onto the elevator before she noticed them and then cordially allowed them to step out first.

"Thank you," they both said as they exited the elevator and started looking for the main hospital check-in. Adam turned and saw the woman enter the elevator with great urgency.

Gee, I hope that lady is okay.

After checking in, Kate was immediately placed in a room where they started monitoring the contractions, along with her vitals and the baby's. Her doctor came in shortly thereafter.

"Hey, Kate!" Dr. Wyatt said in her usual cheery voice. "How's it going?"

Kate was only able to conjure a crooked smile and a thumbs-up.

The doctor chuckled. "Yep, that sounds about right. How long have you been having contractions?"

"Since early this morning."

Dr. Wyatt's eyes widened. "Wow! That long?"

Kate nodded. "At first, I thought it was just cramps or digestive trouble like I've been having, but they started getting worse."

"You look really pale, Kate." She looked at her with concern. "Have you eaten today?"

"No." She shook her head. "Not since the pain started."

"That's probably it then. Let's check your progress, though." She turned and began examining the numbers on the screen. "Well, your vitals all seem within normal range, and the baby's vitals are fine too. How close are the contractions?"

Adam chimed in, "About every ten minutes." He looked at Kate and could tell she was impressed.

"Very good, Daddy," the doctor said and nudged him on the shoulder.

Daddy... Adam thought ...*Holy crap! I'm going to have a kid today!*

The doctor looked at Kate. "I am going to check your cervix now to see how dilated you are."

"Okay," Kate nodded. She laid back and waited.

"Well," the doctor announced upon completion, "looks like you're between five and six centimeters."

Kate looked disappointed.

"Well, what does that mean?" Adam asked.

The doctor turned to Adam. "That just means it'll probably be a few more hours. And she's already tired." Then she turned to Kate. "The good news is that everything looks fine right now. We just have to hang in there for a while longer. In the meantime, do you want something for the pain?"

Kate's mind flashed back for just a moment.

Pain. She pictured her foster dad from when she was nine years old—one of many. He was standing at the top of the stairs with his belt in his hands. He'd just beaten her for letting the dog out without his leash. She was in the bathroom crying and assessing the damage, hoping it wasn't severe enough to keep her home from school the next day.

"It's not too bad," Kate answered.

Chapter 46

As soon as Daphne arrived at the hospital ED, she looked for the first available parking spot, not thinking about how far she'd need to walk. She clip-clopped at breakneck speed from the car, into the building, and then over to the help desk.

"Excuse me," she said urgently to the young man that was checking people in.

"Can I help you?" he asked nonchalantly, chewing a piece of gum. His hair was in dreadlocks and pulled back into a ponytail.

"I'm looking for Renee Weavers. She was checked in already."

"Are you a relative?"

She sighed. *Screw it!* "Yes, I'm her daughter."

He typed Renee's name into the system and located her instantly. "She's in room 404. You'll need a sticker. Hang on, it's printing now."

Hurry up! Hurry up! Hurry up!

Ten seconds later, he ripped the sticker from the machine and handed it to Daphne.

"Thank you," she said as she grabbed it. She strutted through the double doors and began following the signs for the elevator. As she walked, she pulled the paper off the back of her sticker and put it on carelessly. She looked around for a garbage bin but didn't see one. So she crumpled the paper into a ball and shoved it in her handbag. Finally, she found the elevator and pushed the Up button. Again, she waited.

Come on!

The doors opened. She was about to step inside but quickly noticed a young couple, who were expecting, about to exit the elevator.

She's probably in labor. Let her out. Be cool.

The couple stepped out of the elevator and thanked her.

"No problem." Daphne said and waved. As soon as they were out, she darted into the elevator and hit "4."

Once again, the elevator ride seemed to take forever. She gulped and breathed deeply.

She's going to be okay. Don't worry. She's going to be okay.

When the doors opened, she saw a sign indicating to go left for rooms 400 through 410. She turned the corner and saw Julie standing in the hallway. She clip-clopped all the way down to where she was standing. "Julie!" she called. "I'm here."

Julie had been pacing. She stopped and reached out to grab Daphne's arms. "Thank God you're here. The doctor is in with her. Sit down for a minute." She guided her to a double chair just outside the room.

"Just…start from the beginning, Julie. What happened?"

Julie sighed. "So I went to the house to have tea with Renee, like I always do."

Tea? I didn't even know she liked tea.

"I rang the bell and she didn't answer. But the car was in the driveway, so I figured she was home. I got worried, so I used the key that she'd given me when I watched her cats the last time she was on vacation."

"And?" Daphne asked anxiously.

"She was asleep on the couch, or so I thought. I went over to her and tapped her a few times. I said her name really loud, and she didn't wake up, but she was still breathing. I called 9-1-1 right away, and they came to get her. I rode in the back of the ambulance. I would have called you sooner, Daphne, but the dispatcher kept me on the phone until the EMTs arrived. Then the EMTs had a million questions for me on the way here. It wasn't until she was admitted that I actually got a chance to call."

"It's okay," said Daphne. "You did the right thing. Thank you. Thank you for calling 9-1-1 and then me. You probably saved her life."

"I just wish I could have done more," Julie said as she leaned back in her seat and wiped her tears.

Just then, a woman's voice was heard from a few yards away. "Daphne?"

Daphne and Julie turned to see who had spoken. Daphne recognized her instantly. It was Pearl, the nurse from the oncology wing who had been so sweet to Renee. She walked over to them. "I just finished my shift, and someone told me Renee was checked in. What's wrong with my Nene?"

"She's in a coma," Daphne answered, standing up.

Pearl nodded. She did not appear surprised. Then she took a deep breath and said, "Daphne, there's something you need to know." She looked at Julie, as if to suggest that they needed privacy.

"I'll go take a walk," Julie said. She rubbed Daphne's shoulder and ambled down the hall.

Pearl smiled as she passed by. "Thank you."

When they were alone, Daphne crossed her arms. "What the hell is going on? This feels like the *Twilight Zone*! Yesterday, Renee was fine. And now *this*?"

"She's not fine, Daphne," Pearl said. "She hasn't been fine since she left here in November."

"What are you talking about?" she said angrily. "I've seen her almost once a week for *months*! She's eating like normal. She's exercising. She's been her normal self again! In fact, *better* than normal!"

"She's doing those things because she wants to enjoy herself... for as long as she can."

"What are you saying?" Daphne asked weakly.

Pearl took a step closer and placed her hands on Daphne's shoulders. "I'm saying, when she left the hospital, it wasn't because her cancer was gone. It was because she was tired of the treatment. You saw her. She couldn't eat. She couldn't sleep. She was in constant pain. That's no way to live!"

Daphne burst into tears. She sat down again. "So you guys just let her *go*?

Pearl sat down in the chair beside her. "Patients exercise their own free will, Daphne. All we can do is give the diagnosis and offer treatment. The rest is up to them."

"So where was the cancer? When she was scanned in November, where was the cancer?"

Pearl stared at Daphne. "It was in her brain."

Chapter 47

After Deborah had stormed out, Rachel sat at the kitchen table by herself for a while. She was shaken by the fight that ensued, but it hadn't broken her. She was still breathing. She had started making her way "through the swamp." Now she had to go all the way through it. She knew exactly what she needed to do.

She marched upstairs to her bedroom. She walked over to the dresser, where she kept her jewelry box. Then she opened it and pulled out the necklace. She put it in her pocket, went back downstairs, and got in her car.

As she drove, Rachel's heart thumped loudly. Her hands shook. She began to sweat. The stereo was off. Her thoughts raced like never before, mostly about how tired she was of being angry. She'd been angry at the man who'd killed her father—who would die in prison. She'd been angry at Mr. Marshall for abusing her and Baylee. For so long, she had wanted him to pay for what he did. Her silence, however, made that impossible. It had also created a situation where *she* was paying for his crimes by suffering for so long. It wasn't fair, and it wasn't fair to continue being angry with her mother either.

Rachel began to realize that deep down, it really came down to fear, especially where her mother was concerned. Somewhere in her heart she believed that if she allowed herself to love and be loved by her mother again, she'd end up disappointed.

Suddenly, a voice from within came through and spoke the truth. *Let's face it—you've given her plenty of reasons to give up on you, and she hasn't. What does that tell you?*

She realized then and there how foolish she had been.

By now, Rachel had arrived at a pier. She parked her car and turned off the engine. As she stepped out of her car and looked out onto the water, she could see how the afternoon sun danced on the surface. She closed her eyes and heard the sounds of the seagulls and pelicans. She could smell the saltiness in the air. As she looked around, she noticed that there were no people around. *It's perfect.*

She pulled the necklace out of her pocket and clasped it in her hand firmly. Taking a deep breath, she began walking the path down to the edge of the pier. She looked down. The wood beneath her feet looked just like the wood that had been used to build the deck behind the Marshalls' house, making the location even more fitting. She looked farther down and could see the water moving about and splashing upward, leaving drops of water on the boards. It made her think about life. Like that water, it is always moving, even if we're not. For over twenty years, life had been happening all around her, and she'd been missing it.

When she reached the edge of the pier, she could see the panoramic view of the large body of water. It had no end. It stretched out as far as the eye could see, and then it just went on. Again...life. It just keeps going.

She sat down on one of the benches and opened her hand. Staring at the necklace with the "—ST—ENDS" charm, she knew there was one more thing she had to do before she released it. Quickly, she looked around one more time to make sure no one was around... It was just her. She closed her eyes and began to breathe the way Dr. Nova had taught her. With each breath, she began to visualize the backyard of the Marshalls' house.

This time, in her vision, the sun was out. The leaves on the trees and the grass were a vibrant beautiful shade of green. She could see squirrels scampering near the woods. Butterflies were dancing among the flowers. She walked around to the edge of the deck and got down on her hands and knees. There was Baylee. This time, she wasn't hugging herself, rocking back and forth. She was drawing in the sand with a stick.

In her vision, Rachel crawled over to where the little girl was sitting. "Hi, Baylee."

"Hi," Baylee answered. Her voice was still somber but noticeably more content than in Rachel's last vision.

"I'm sorry I had to leave the last time. I wish I could have stayed and helped you."

Baylee sighed. "That's okay." She continued to draw in the sand.

"Remember the last time I was here? How I said the things your dad does are not your fault?"

"Mm-hm." Baylee nodded.

"Do you believe me?"

She shrugged.

"Well, I'm going to tell you something else, and I really hope you listen."

Baylee looked at Rachel in the eye studiously.

"He is a *liar*. He tells you that if you tell, something worse will happen, right?"

Baylee looked as if she might cry.

"Don't believe him! He's a coward! Anyone who abuses children and then tells them to keep quiet is a no-good coward! Do you understand?"

Slowly, she nodded.

"You need to take your power back. Stop hiding, Baylee. If you tell your mom, she'll believe you. She *will* protect you. She *will* make sure it stops. I'm sure of it."

"How do you know?" Baylee asked.

Rachel paused. "Because *I'm* a mommy, and that's what mommies do. We protect our children. We just need to know what's going on."

"Will I ever see you again?"

Rachel pressed her lips together. "I don't know. Maybe."

Baylee sat up on her knees and inched closer. She threw her arms around Rachel's neck and hugged her. Rachel wrapped her arms around the little girl and held her.

"It's okay," she whispered, gently rocking back and forth. "Everything is going to be okay."

"How about me?" a different voice said suddenly.

Rachel let go of Baylee and looked behind her to where she'd heard the voice coming from. To her disbelief, she was looking at herself—her seven-year-old self. She was sitting in the dirt just a couple of feet away.

"You?" Rachel said. "You are going to be okay also."

The seven-year-old Rachel sat up straighter and listened.

"You are going to have an amazing life. You'll have a wonderful husband and two beautiful kids. You're going to be *better* than okay."

The little girl crawled over to her, and they hugged.

Rachel suddenly opened her eyes and realized she was hugging herself. She was still at the pier. The water in front of her splashed loudly.

She sighed deeply, stood up, and stepped up to the farthest edge of the pier, where she could drop the necklace into the water. She opened her palm and looked at it one more time. Then she extended her arm so that the necklace was hovering over the water. She closed her eyes. *Take your power back.* She released the necklace and opened her eyes so that she could watch it fall. It hit the water with a tiny splash...and then it disappeared.

Chapter 48

For the next couple of hours, Kate's contractions continued to intensify and come closer together. Her doctor and a couple of nurses took turns coming in every so often to check how dilated she was. When she was at about seven centimeters, the doctor asked one more time if she wanted pain medication. "There's no sense being in pain, Kate. It's perfectly safe for the baby. Are you sure you don't want the epidural?

"I'm sure," she said, lying on her side with her eyes half shut.

"Can I have one?" Adam joked. His hands were sore from Kate squeezing them during contractions.

The doctor winked at him. "Hang in there, champ. I'll check on you again in a little while." She left.

The room was quiet except for the sounds coming from the monitors and Kate's breathing. "I didn't think it would take this long," she said in exhaustion.

Adam rubbed her back.

"You've been great."

He smiled.

She turned over onto her side and faced him. "I've never been so tired in my whole life," she whispered.

Adam stroked her hair gently. He was speechless.

"Thank you," she said, looking into his kind brown eyes.

"For what?"

She shrugged. "Being here, I guess."

"I had nowhere else to be."

She laughed a little. Then the smile began to fade.

"What's wrong?" he asked.

"I don't know." She shut her eyes, like she was in pain. "I'm just getting that feeling again."

Suddenly, one of the monitors started beeping loudly, and some of the numbers flashed yellow. Before Adam or Kate could push the Help button, there was a nurse walking in.

"What's going on?" Adam asked.

The nurse examined the monitor. "The baby's heart rate is dropping."

Kate rolled onto her back. "Is she going to be okay?"

"Hang on," the nurse said.

They watched the monitor for about ten seconds. The numbers turned green again, and the beeping stopped.

The nurse sighed. "We're good." She tapped Kate on the foot.

Adam exhaled loudly and leaned forward with his head between his knees.

"Thank God," Kate whispered, clenching her chest.

"Let me get the doctor," the nurse said as she turned to leave.

Adam sat in the chair beside Kate. "That scared the crap out of me."

"Me too."

Dr. Wyatt came in, smiling as usual, though this time it wasn't quite so big. "I heard we had a little action in here."

Kate pointed to the monitor. "The baby's heart rate was dropping."

The doctor reviewed the printed sheet that was coming out of the machine. "Looks like her oxygen was getting low as well."

Adam gulped.

"Kate," the doctor asked. "It seems okay right now, but we're not out of the woods yet. This could be a sign that the baby is in distress and there's at least the possibility that a C-section may be needed, especially since you're not at ten centimeters yet."

Adam stood up. "Well, can we wait a little longer before we do that?"

Dr. Wyatt looked at Kate and then back at Adam. "I'm sorry to bring this up, but are you guys married?"

"No," said Kate softly, "we're not."

"Sorry, Adam," the doctor said. "It's going to have to be Kate's decision."

He looked at Kate and then at the doctor. "Well, I guess you don't need me in here." He walked out and began pacing down the hall.

Once alone, Dr. Wyatt sat down at Kate's bedside, getting eye level with her patient. "I'm sorry. I didn't mean to upset him."

"It's okay," she said softly.

"Kate, here are the options. I can give you Pitocin to speed up the labor so that you can deliver sooner. The other option is to just go ahead and do the C-section."

"What are the risks?"

"Well," the doctor said gently, "when we speed up labor, it may slow down the baby's heart rate again. If it gets too low or if that happens too often, it's not good for her."

"And the C-section?"

"Well, it *is* a surgical procedure, so it comes with a greater risk to *you*."

Kate swallowed.

The doctor continued, "You're almost at forty weeks, so the risk of harm to the baby with a C-section is minimal. It's *you* I'm worried about."

In the hallway, Adam had found a bench to sit on, far enough away that he couldn't hear what Kate and Dr. Wyatt were discussing. He didn't want to know what they were discussing. If he knew, he'd want to give his opinion.

It's not up to you, man! It's her decision.

That's my kid too! Don't I get some say in what happens?

She's not going to do anything that puts the baby at risk.

"Excuse me, young man," a male voice said.

Adam looked up and saw a man in his seventies standing next to the bench where he was sitting.

"Mind if I sit down?"

Adam nodded.

"Thanks." He smiled and sat down beside him. He extended his hand. "My name's Paul."

"Adam." They shook hands.

"Nice to meet you, Adam." They sat in awkward silence for a moment. "Uh, may I ask why a healthy young man like you looks so distraught?"

Adam turned to him. "I'm not sure it would make sense to you."

"Try me." Paul elbowed Adam.

He struggled for the words to begin. "Well, for starters, I have a kid that's about to be born."

"That's great—" Paul immediately stopped himself. "Has there been a complication?"

Adam nodded. "You could say that, and I'm scared about what's going to happen."

"To the baby or your wife?"

"We're not married." Adam quickly corrected him. "In fact, we're not even really *together*, but I love her." He swallowed. "And I just don't think we're going to see the situation the same way."

"How so?"

Adam stood up and paced.

"It's okay, son. You can tell me. I won't judge. Hell, I'll probably never see you again!"

He stopped walking and looked at Paul. "I just can't help but think if something happens to the baby"—he looked down—"Kate could always have another one." He sat down again. "But if something happens to Kate, that's it. She's gone." He looked at Paul, trying not to cry. "I can't replace her."

"And you can't replace that kid either," Paul said.

"Is it shitty that I feel this way?"

"Like I said, kid, I won't judge. It makes sense that you'd feel that way."

"Yeah, but will it make sense to *her*?"

Paul laughed a little and patted him on the back. "Damned if I know what makes sense to a woman, especially a mother."

Adam stood back up. "Well, thanks for the talk. I guess I'd better go talk to her."

"You do that, son." Paul waved. "And good luck."

Adam took two steps and stopped. *Ugh! You turd! You didn't ask him if he's okay. Maybe he has a sick family member or something.* He turned around to face Paul again. "By the way, why are *you* here?"

"Me?" Paul asked in a voice that sounded almost astonished. He became pensive for a moment. Then he answered, "Strange thing, really. I had just left a support group meeting and was about to go home, but something told me that I should come *here* instead... almost like someone *needed* me."

Although Adam did not fully comprehend what Paul meant, he nodded and smiled before he walked away.

Back in the room, Kate was by herself, staring at the ceiling.

"Hey," Adam whispered.

"Hey." She didn't look at him.

"So...what did the doctor say?"

Kate turned her head and looked at him. "She said we could speed up the labor, which might put the baby at risk...or we can go ahead and do the C-section."

"What do you want to do?"

She leaned closer to Adam. The look in her eyes intensified. "I want to do whatever gives this baby the best chance."

Adam sat down. "Kate—"

"Adam," she cut him off, "you said you love me, right?"

He nodded.

"If that's true, then listen to me. I'm telling you, something is definitely wrong. I don't know what, but I feel it in my gut. They need to take her out as soon as possible."

Adam froze.

"Get her out!" she said urgently.

Chapter 49

Daphne was still standing in the hallway with Pearl. She was still in shock over what she'd learned. Renee's oncologist came out of the room.

"Dr. Wallace," Daphne said as soon as she saw him. She remembered him well from all the time she'd previously spent in the hospital with Renee. "Is she okay?"

He sighed. "She doesn't seem to be waking up from her coma. It might be good for her to hear your voice."

She looked him in the eye and opened her mouth to speak, but she quickly stopped herself. *It's no use, Daphne. He's not going to tell you anything you don't already know.* Somberly, she walked into the room.

Renee was hooked up to seemingly every machine known to mankind. Her breathing was slow but steady, and every once in a while, one of her fingers would twitch ever so slightly.

Daphne's heart broke. *Not again.* She pulled a nearby chair up so that she can sit right next to her. "The doctor said you could hear my voice. If that's true, open your eyes."

There was no response.

"You're probably mad at me," Daphne said, trying to lighten the moment. "You probably heard through the grapevine that I posted that video trying to find my birth mom."

Again, there was no response. Even the twitching of Renee's fingers had stopped.

"Well, if it makes you feel better, she hasn't responded. Serves me right, huh? I've been an idiot during this whole thing. For two years, I obsessed over what I'd do if I lost you. Then I wasted time trying to find a way to somehow make it easier if I did lose you. That whole time, I should've just been with you. I should have just told you that I love you. I should've told you that no matter *who* gave birth to me, *you're* the person that's been there for me…more than *anyone*." She grabbed Renee's hand and squeezed it. "And that's why you have to wake up, because I need to tell you all of those things, and I need to know that *you* know."

Renee was quiet and still.

Daphne began to cry softly.

Suddenly, Renee squeezed her hand.

Daphne looked up.

Renee's eyes were opening. They looked tired but peaceful. Her breathing became heavier, like she was exerting herself.

"Hey," Daphne said, reaching up to stroke her hair.

"Hey, baby," Renee whispered. It was clear she was having trouble speaking. Her breathing was shallow.

Daphne leaned in so she could hear her better.

"Everything…is going…to be…okay," she said softly between breaths.

Suddenly, a loud noise blared from one of the machines. Daphne dropped Renee's hand from being startled. The doctor came charging in, along with two other nurses.

"What's going on?" Daphne demanded.

The doctor didn't answer. He immediately looked at Renee and then at the monitor. Then he looked at one of the nurses soberly and said, "Get her out!" He was talking about Daphne. The nurse began to tug at Daphne's arm to lead her out of the room.

"What? I'm not going anywhere!"

"Get her out, I said!" yelled the doctor.

"This is my mother! You're not taking me anywhere!"

But she had no choice. Both nurses had her now, one by each arm. They were physically dragging her out of the room.

"That's my mom! You can't make me leave!" she yelled in the hallway. Other people were staring, and for once, Daphne didn't care.

"Daphne!" Pearl appeared and grabbed her by the shoulders. "You straighten out, young lady!" She urged in her toughest voice. "Pull yourself together! Your mama raised you better than that!"

Daphne breathed loudly, trying to calm down. Tears rolled down her cheeks.

Pearl turned and walked over to the nearest nurse's station to get Daphne a tissue. By the time she returned, Daphne was gone.

Chapter 50

When Rachel got back to her car, the inside was stifling from the heat. She quickly turned on the engine and started the AC. Then she checked her phone. She had missed a call from Deborah. For a moment, her habit of always ignoring her calls and messages began to creep its way in, but she fought it. She took a deep breath and dialed.

"Hello," Deborah said when she answered. Her voice sounded like she'd been crying.

"Hey, I just saw that you called."

"Thank you for calling me back."

Rachel listened quietly.

"I just wanted to apologize for rushing out the way that I did. You deserve better from me."

Rachel sighed. "I get it."

"And I really don't have any excuse for the past other than the fact that when your dad died, I was a mess. I loved him very much, and he was too young to die. Plus, I never expected to be a single mom. I was scared. I was overwhelmed. I just didn't know what to do half the time."

Rachel wiped a tear off her cheek.

"But please believe me when I tell you I love you. I always have and I always will. And if I'd known what was happening back then, I *never* would have made you go back."

"I believe you, Mom." She sniffed

"Thank you, sweetie," Deborah said in a weak voice. "And I really don't know where to go from here, but I'd like to try."

Rachel took a deep breath. "Well, for starters, would like to meet your grandkids sometime?"

Deborah's tears of sadness became tears of joy. "Yes!" she exclaimed happily. "Yes, I would like that very much!"

"Great," Rachel said. "I promise I'll call you soon, and we'll figure out when."

"Sounds good," she said. "I'll talk to you later."

"Okay," said Rachel. "Bye, Mom."

"Bye," Deborah said and hung up. She, too, was sitting in her car. After hanging up, she raised her head and looked out the driver's side window. On the other side of the street, she could see a house. The house had siding that was at least twenty years old and was badly in need of a pressure wash. The small garden in the front yard that was once a home to beautiful yellow and purple flowers was nothing more than a pile of dirt surrounded by brown grass. Even from the street, Deborah could see that ugly grass extending all the way into the backyard. And in that backyard, attached to the back of the house, was a large wooden deck.

She had been staring at the house for nearly an hour. Several times, she'd contemplated getting out of her car and knocking on the front door. But she knew she had to be careful. She had to be steadfast. She had to have it all planned out ahead of time.

"Not today," she whispered to herself. Then she put the car in drive and drove away.

Chapter 51

It didn't take long for the doctors to prep for Kate's C-section. The shiny metal from the surgical tools nearly blinded her as they wheeled her in. Two of the nurses carefully helped her onto the operating table. Then they gently turned her to her side long enough to inject her with the anesthesia. She slowly rolled onto her back and tried to make herself as comfortable as she could.

"Now remember, Kate," Dr. Wyatt said, "that won't make you go to sleep. It'll just numb the pain. You can see the baby when she's born."

Kate smiled weakly. She was beyond exhausted from the long labor. In fact, she was so tired that as the doctors began working, she drifted off the sleep, dreaming once again.

It was her second-grade field trip to the aquarium. Kate was standing in front of the tank that held the giant octopus. Its tentacles danced gracefully in a swarm of bubbles.

Ms. Frances was beside her. "Do you remember what makes the octopus so special?"

Kate answered, "It has three hearts."

"That's right!" Her teacher beamed. "What else?"

There was a silence. Kate stared at the octopus. For a moment, she even believed that the octopus was staring at her. Yet she wasn't afraid. The answer came to her. "The mother octopus is the best mother in the world."

Ms. Frances probed excitedly, "Yes! Now why? What makes them the best mothers?"

Kate continued to gaze upon the octopus and recited the facts from their science lesson. "Well, they lay their eggs and they have to watch them for fifty-three months." She paused and turned to her teacher briefly. "That's more than four years!"

Ms. Frances chuckled. "It's a long, long time, isn't it? And what does she do during that long time?"

Kate's glance returned to the animal. "She doesn't think about herself. She doesn't eat. She doesn't sleep. She has to make sure that her babies get enough oxygen to breathe. She protects them from other animals that want to eat them. It's really, really hard work."

"And then?" asked Ms. Frances.

Kate looked sad. "Then she dies." She tipped her head and frowned. She looked at her teacher. "Why do they have to die, Ms. Frances? It's not fair."

Ms. Frances knelt down, getting eye level with her student. Gently, she brushed back the piece of hair that was in the child's face and tucked it behind her ear. "Sweetie, every creature in this world has a purpose, and each one's is different." She pointed to the octopus. "This one's purpose is to bring her offspring into the world, so once she serves her purpose, her time in the world is done. They die so that their babies can live. There's no greater sacrifice for a mother to make."

In the OR, Kate opened her eyes. Although she could see clearly and knew where she was, it felt as if her mind was somewhere else. She couldn't feel her body. She looked around and noticed that one of the nurses had tears in her eyes. *Is she crying because she's happy or sad?*

Dr. Wyatt was saying something, but it was hard to make out. Kate tried to raise her head so she could listen better, but it felt like it weighed a hundred pounds.

Suddenly, a voice from inside spoke to her. It was a voice she'd never heard before, yet there was something familiar and comforting about it. "Look," it whispered. "Look at her."

Her eyes moved from left to right. Her head only moved slightly. Finally, she was able to lower her glance to her chest. She flinched.

There was her baby resting on her chest peacefully. She was swaddled in a hospital blanket with a beanie cap on her tiny head. She was the most beautiful baby Kate had ever seen. There was no movement.

Oh, God! She's not moving. Kate panicked. *Is she okay?*

"She's perfect," one of the nurses whispered. "You did it."

Suddenly, Kate began to relax again. She looked closer and saw the steady rise and fall of the baby's breathing. "She's okay," Kate whispered out loud. "She's okay. Thank you…"

Then Kate closed her eyes again.

For the last time.

Chapter 52

After disappearing on Pearl, Daphne ran to the door that led to the stairway and down the steps. She opened the door on the first floor and turned down the hallway—to the chapel. She walked inside and found that it was empty. There was a giant cross on the wall directly in front of her. Leaning against that same wall, there was a table filled with candles that people had lit for their loved ones.

As Daphne approached the table, hugging herself, she noticed that on a perpendicular wall, there was a framed print of The Serenity Prayer. She felt a chill. *That's the same prayer they said the first night I went to an ACDP meeting.* She stared blankly at it for an undetermined amount of time.

When she stopped staring, she shook her head and focused her attention on the candles. There was a long one in the middle that towered above all the other ones. Daphne could only assume that it was the one used to light the others. She looked around and found one that had not been lit, right in the front row on the far left. Carefully, she took the longest candle out of its holder, used it to light a candle for Renee, and then replaced it. Standing right there in front of the cross, she closed her eyes and prayed.

I know I'm not the most deserving person in the world, and I know I haven't prayed to you in a really long time. I'm sorry about that. And I know the situation seems completely hopeless, but you know what they say, 'Miracles happen every day."...I guess that's what I need...I need a miracle. I don't feel like I can make it without her. Please, please help me.

Daphne began to feel as if someone was watching her. She opened her eyes and slowly turned around to face the entrance. It turned out someone *was* watching her. He was standing in the doorway. His eyes were red from crying. It was Brock.

When they saw each other, he started walking toward her. Daphne met him halfway, in the middle of the chapel between the aisles.

They stood face-to-face with one foot of space between them.

"What are you doing here?" Daphne asked, trying not to cry.

"Renee tried to call me this morning. It's not like her to do that. She didn't leave a message, so I called her back. She didn't answer, so I tried calling you, but you didn't answer."

"Why didn't you leave a message?"

Brock huffed. "What good would that have done? You've never returned one of my calls before."

Daphne lowered her head, realizing again how foolish she'd been.

"Anyway, I drove all day until I got to Renee's house. One of the neighbors saw me and asked if I was looking for Renee. She told me there'd been an ambulance there, so I came straight here."

"How did you know I was in the chapel?"

Brock hesitated. "I checked in downstairs, and they told me the room number. And when I got up there, they told me what happened."

Daphne's posture changed. She looked like a lioness about to jump at her prey. "If you're about to tell me...that she died...when *you* were the one that left us all those years ago..."

"I never wanted this for her, Daphne. I swear. Just because our marriage didn't work out doesn't mean I wished anything bad on her. She was a good person."

"Don't you tell me she died!" she yelled and burst into tears. "Shut up! Just shut up!"

Brock stepped forward and hugged her. "I'm sorry," he whispered.

Her body went limp as she sobbed. "No! Don't say that! She's okay! She has to be okay!" She carried on for several minutes.

Brock held her the entire time.

Chapter 53

"Watch me, Daddy!" Avery yelled from the top of the playset at the park.

Lee pushed Nick gently in his bucket swing while he kept an eye on his almost-four-year-old. "Okay," he said for the third time in a row. His cell phone began to vibrate. He removed it from his pocket and saw that Rachel had just sent a text message: "Hey. I've got dinner covered, so don't worry about it."

Avery noticed the look of surprise on her father's face and walked up to him. "What's going on, Daddy?"

Lee put the phone back in his pocket. "I was just reading a message from Mommy. She said she's making dinner for us tonight, so Daddy doesn't have to cook."

"Yay!" said Avery. She ran off to climb the stairs of the playset again.

* * *

Rachel, who had gone back to the grocery store for a few more items, walked into the kitchen and placed the bags carefully on the counter. Her hands shook. "You can do this," she said to herself. "It's been a trying day, but you can do this."

She huffed loudly and got to work. In a mixing bowl, she combined two pounds of lean ground beef, minced garlic, salt, pepper, and oregano. While she worked the mixture, her knuckles began to ache from the cold meat. But she didn't stop until it was evenly blended and ready to roll into meatballs. Next, she flipped over one of the now-empty trays from the ground beef and placed one meatball on it. Over and over, she repeated the process until all of the mixture had been used up.

Next, she took out a large deep skillet, set it on top of the stove, and turned on the heat. She added olive oil and waited until it was nice and hot before dropping in the meatballs. They sizzled when they hit the pan. The scent of oil and garlic tickled the inside of Rachel's nose. She inhaled it deeply and found it surprisingly comforting.

Finally, she reached under the counter by the sink and took out the biggest pot she could find. She filled the pot with water, added salt, and placed it on the burner beside the sizzling meatballs. Her heart pounded a little harder. Slowly, she turned the burner on high and waited.

Soon the water began to boil, and Rachel added the final ingredient for her family's dinner.

At that moment, the front door opened. Avery was the first to charge through the door, remove her shoes, and run toward the kitchen.

"Don't run, Avery," Lee said. He took off his shoes plus Nick's and followed Avery into the kitchen. Nick, who had recently learned to walk, held his hand, and they moved at a snail's pace. When they entered the kitchen, Lee's mouth dropped open. The smell was unmistakable. He looked around at the evidence—the meatballs that Rachel had just set aside to cool, marinara being poured into a saucepan to be warmed, and the pasta that boiled on top of the stove.

"Daddy!" Avery jumped up and down. "We're having *spaghetti!*"

Lee, who stood speechless, let go of Nick's hand. Nick toddled toward his mother. Rachel scooped up her son and held him tenderly while he rested his head on her shoulder. Avery wrapped her arms around Rachel's legs and hugged her as tightly as she could. "Mmm! I love you, Mommy!"

"I love *you*," said Rachel. Her eyes and Lee's were locked on each other.

Chapter 54

D r. Wyatt came out of the OR, appearing exhausted.

Adam, who had been pacing up and down the hallway, stopped and walked over to her. "How did it go in there?"

"Congratulations," she said softly. "You have a beautiful, healthy baby girl."

Adam sighed loudly with relief. "How's Kate?"

Dr. Wyatt put her hand on Adam's shoulder. With her head, she motioned toward the chairs that were against a nearby wall. "Let's sit down."

Adam's stomach was suddenly in knots. He sat down. Dr. Wyatt sat beside him.

"Adam," she said somberly. "Kate didn't make it."

His eyes widened. "What do you mean?" He stood up and started to back away from her.

"Try to stay calm," she said. "The good news is that we saved your daughter."

Adam's vision became blurry. He rubbed his eyes. "I don't understand… What happened in there?"

Dr. Wyatt's face dropped. "She was really weak, and she lost too much blood. We did everything we could."

Adam began pacing again. He couldn't look at the doctor, who was trying to explain the horrific ordeal.

"This happens sometimes with C-sections. Rarely, mind you, but it does happen. People with certain medical conditions are more at risk than others…but since we didn't know her family history, we didn't know her risk factors."

"It's my fault," he declared, sitting back down. "If I hadn't gotten her pregnant, she'd still be alive."

"Adam," Dr. Wyatt tried to comfort him, "please don't beat yourself up. These things just happen sometimes."

"Dr. Wyatt?" a nurse said, peeking her head out from inside the operating room.

The doctor looked at the nurse and then at Adam. "She has something that might make you feel better." She stood up, walked over to the nurse, and carefully took a swaddled bundle from her arms. "Thank you," she whispered.

Adam froze. He was fairly certain he knew what Dr. Wyatt was referring to.

She approached and gently handed him his newborn daughter. "This is your baby," she said quietly but excitedly.

He carefully put one hand behind the spot where her neck and head met and the other hand under her bottom. For the first time, he looked at his child. She had the tiniest button nose, rosy heart-shaped lips, and her skin was the color of porcelain. Her thin, jet-black hair poked through the bottom of the beanie cap that had been placed on her head. His eyes welled up with tears.

She looks just like Kate.

Chapter 55

It was 8:00 p.m. Ray pulled his metallic green Prius into the driveway and parked it behind his wife's PT Cruiser. He had been teaching since early that morning and was looking forward to spending time with her. He breathed in the salty sea air deeply and then exhaled. *Ah, home at last.*

As he turned the knob and pushed the door open, he heard a familiar sound. His wife, Mila, was at the piano playing "Moonlight Sonata." There was a glass of wine on top of the piano and a look of melancholy on her face. *Uh-oh. She's sad.*

He set his briefcase down on the floor in a corner and hung his keys on a wall mount near the door. Then he walked over to the piano and sat next to his wife. "Hey." He put his arm around her and kissed her temple.

"Hey." Mila smiled bravely and continued playing.

"Did you have your last session with a patient today."

She stopped playing for a moment. "No, but I don't think it'll be long before she no longer needs me. She's making remarkable progress." She resumed playing.

"Do you want to talk about it?"

"You know I can't. Confidentiality."

"I know. I mean, about how you're feeling."

Mila stopped playing again. This time she reached for her glass of wine and took a sip. She sighed deeply. "It just never gets easier. No matter how many times I meet a new patient, get to know them, watch their progress, and then celebrate that progress, it never gets easier when they leave."

"Well, you know what I'm always telling you about that."

Mila nodded and placed her elbow on the piano, her hand cradling her forehead. "You always tell me that the fact that they're moving on means I've done my job."

"Exactly. And you do it damn well."

"There's just also that part of me that thinks if they stay..."

"It's because they like you."

She nodded.

"Babe," he said, hugging her tightly, "I'm sure they like you. But you've got to remember that the therapy is for *them*."

"I know. Trust me, I know how silly it sounds. I'm a grown woman and I still want people to like me. It's like being friends with everybody at school but never being invited to their birthday parties."

Ray gently turned her chin toward himself so that he could look into her eyes. "That's why you're so good at what you do, because you care so much."

"And that's also why it hurts so much. It's kind of a double-edged sword."

"Let me ask you a question. If you could choose between not caring at all or continuing to feel what you feel, what would you choose?"

"You're psychoanalyzing me now?" Mila giggled.

Ray laughed too. "Hey, after fifteen years of marriage, it was bound to happen."

"Maybe I should start teaching your classes then."

"Dr. Nova, you're avoiding the question."

"Shut up!" She laughed again and nudged him playfully.

"Well?"

She thought long and hard before answering. "I'd choose...to be exactly the way I am. I mean, it sucks feeling so much, caring so much, hurting so much, but if I couldn't feel that, I wouldn't feel the good stuff either. In fact, sometimes the bad stuff makes the good stuff that much better, just by sheer comparison."

"There you go," Ray said.

"I mean, isn't that what life is all about? The experience? Good, bad, or whatever?" She took another sip of wine. The enthusiasm in her voice grew. "It's all part of the human experience. And in the end, something beautiful can come out of every situation, no matter how sad it seems at first. I wouldn't want to miss any of it."

"Well, my dear, I believe you just had a 'watershed' moment."

"Thank you, Professor Nova." She winked at her husband.

Four Years Later...

Chapter 56

M rs. Keegan circulated the preschool classroom as her students worked on their drawings. The assignment was for each child to make a picture of his or her family. The short rectangular tables were covered with white paper and buckets of crayons. Each table had four to five chairs whose bottoms rested about one foot off the floor. The children worked diligently and cheerfully. Each time a student tired of working with one color, he or she dropped it into a nearby bucket and reached for another with careful thought.

One particular student was making a drawing that caught Mrs. Keegan's attention.

It showed a little girl (no doubt the artist herself) with a woman standing inside a house. There was a man standing outside the house. There were two clouds at the top of the page, one in the left corner and one in the right. On each cloud was a figure of a woman with wings and a halo.

"That's a nice drawing," Mrs. Keegan said as she knelt beside the child.

"Thank you," she answered politely. She tucked a piece of her dark-brown hair behind her ear, which frequently fell in her face.

"So who are all of these people?" her teacher asked.

The child pointed inside the house. "This is me and my mommy at our house." A brief pause followed. "And this is my daddy coming to see me." She pointed to the man.

"I see," Mrs. Keegan said sweetly. "So you live with Mom, and Dad comes to visit."

"Yes," the little girl answered immediately. "But not at first."

The child's comment confused the teacher, but she knew good and well that home situations were often complicated. She decided to change the subject.

* * *

Meanwhile, that same child's mother was en route to pick her up. She was patiently weathering the afternoon stop-and-go traffic. When the car was not in motion, she propped her left elbow on the door and bobbed her head to the beat of the music coming from the car stereo. Her ponytail bounced to the beat. She tapped the unpolished fingers of her right hand against the steering wheel.

* * *

"What about these people?" Mrs. Keegan asked, pointing to the top of her picture. "Are they in the sky?"

"Uh-huh." The little girl reached for a blue crayon and began filling in the background of her picture.

"Who are they?"

She stopped coloring and pointed to the left cloud. "Well, this is my angel mommy, Kate." Her eyes dropped. "She went to heaven when I was a baby."

"Oh," Mrs. Keegan said, trying to sound upbeat. "Is that why you're named Katie?"

"Yes. Mommy says when she found out who my angel mommy was, she gave me her name."

* * *

Katie's mom had just gotten off the freeway and was turning onto the street that led to the preschool. "Almost there, baby," she muttered aloud. "Mommy's almost there."

* * *

Mrs. Keegan continued asking questions about Katie's interesting picture. "How about this other one?" She pointed to the cloud on the other side.

"That's my mommy's angel. She went to heaven, too, on the same day as my angel. Mommy says they both look after me."

"Well, it sounds like you have a lot of people who love you. You're very lucky."

"I know." She smiled and returned to her coloring.

As Katie was putting the final touches on her picture, her mom parked in front of the preschool. She jumped out of her car, her sneakers hitting the pavement softly. She shut the car door and jogged slowly up to the school entrance. There was another parent coming out, holding her toddler son on her hip. Katie's mom stopped and held the door open for them.

"Thanks." The other mom smiled as she walked by her.

"You're welcome," Katie's mom said. Then she walked up to the window of her daughter's classroom door and watched her for a moment. She had just gotten out of her seat and walked up to her teacher to show off her artwork. Her teacher complimented her on a job well done, and Katie beamed with pride.

Her mom opened the door quietly. "Hi, Mrs. Keegan," she said from the doorway, waiting for her daughter to turn.

Mrs. Keegan answered, "Hey, Daphne."

Katie gasped excitedly and looked at the door. "Mommy!" she cried as she ran to Daphne.

"Hi, baby!" Daphne scooped Katie up and hugged her.

Mrs. Keegan watched the two of them together. Her heart filled with warmth as she witnessed the beautiful bond between a mother and her child.

About the Author

M. L. Curtis has been writing stories and poetry since the age of seven. In college, she earned a degree in Elementary Education and went on to teach children in inner-city schools for over fifteen years. Writing, however, has remained her greatest passion. In 2010, she self-published a children's book entitled *Mice!* (under the name Mel Jorgensen). Eight years after its release, she threw herself into the creative process and completed her first full-length novel, *Layers of Silence*. Her desire to write stems from her desire to reach individuals on a personal level and inspire them to become better, healthier versions of themselves. She currently lives in the beautiful state of North Carolina, where she is married and raising a daughter.

CPSIA information can be obtained
at www.ICGtesting.com
Printed in the USA
FSHW021131080120
65806FS

9 781645 440888